COURIER

FOR

LEE

AND

JACKSON

1861 ~ 1865

MEMOIRS

WALBROOK D. SWANK
COLONEL, USAF RET.

BURD STREET PRESS
DIVISION OF
WHITE MANE PUBLISHING, INC.

Cover Art: Confederate Courier Awaiting Orders
            Culpeper, Virginia September 19, 1863
            Courtesy Library of Congress

Copyright © 1993
By Walbrook D. Swank, Colonel USAF, RET.
Route 2, Box 433
Mineral, Virginia 23117

The acid-free paper used in this book meets the guidelines for permanence and durability of the Committee on Production Guidelines for Book Longevity of the Council of Library Resources.

This Burd Street Press book
was printed by
Beidel Printing House, Inc.
63 West Burd Street
Shippensburg, PA 17257

For a complete list of available publications
please write
Burd Street Press
Division of White Mane Publishing Company, Inc.
P.O. Box 152
Shippensburg, PA 17257

Library of Congress Cataloging-in-Publication Data

Gill, John, 1841-1912.
    Courier for Lee and Jackson : 1861-1865 memoirs / [edited by] Walbrook D. Swank.
        p.   cm.
    Includes bibliographical references (p.) and index.
    ISBN 0-942597-55-9 (alk. paper) : $12.00
    1. Gill, John, 1841-1912. 2. United States--History--Civil War, 1861-1865--Personal narratives, Confederate. 3. Confederate States of America. Army of Northern Virginia--Biography. 4. Soldiers--Confederate States of America--Biography. 5. Confederate States of America--History. I. Swank, Walbrook D. (Walbrook Davis) II. Title.
E605.G467 1993
973.7'455--dc20   93-17531
                                                                        CIP

PRINTED IN THE UNITED STATES OF AMERICA

DEDICATION

to

Marylanders Who Fought
For The Confederacy

About The Author

Since his retirement from the United States Air Force after a distinguished career, which included a short tour of duty at The White House, Colonel Walbrook D. Swank has devoted much time to his hobby, writing about our Southern heritage and history. His grandfather fought under General J.E.B. "JEB" Stuart, Commander of the Cavalry Corps, Army of Northern Virginia, and was a relative of President Jefferson Davis. This is his seventh book relating to the War Between the States. He is a member of the Society of Civil War Historians and the Military Order of the Stars and Bars.

In recognition of the writer's contributions to the preservation and promotion of our Southern heritage and history he has been awarded the Jefferson Davis Medal by the United Daughters of the Confederacy.

The Colonel holds a Masters degree in American Military History and was awarded membership in the Bonnie Blue Society which is based on his scholarly research and published literature.

ALSO BY THE AUTHOR

Clash of Sabres — Blue And Gray

The War And Louisa County, 1861-1865

Eyewitness To War, 1861-1865 — Memoirs of Men Who Fought In The Greatest All Cavalry Battle Of The War

Train Running For The Confederacy — An Eyewitness Memoir

Confederate War Stories, 1861-1865

And the Award Winning Book

Confederate Letters And Diaries, 1861-1865

CONTENTS

ILLUSTRATIONS ————————————

MAPS

INTRODUCTION ———————————————

When the dark clouds of approaching war hovered over the skies of the border state of Maryland on the eve of hostilities and the North-South conflict in 1861, the people of the state were called upon to make a painful choice whether to support the Union or the Confederacy.

Baltimore was the scene of the first bloodshed of the war when, on April 19, 1861, a Massachusetts military unit marched through the town en route to Washington. An angry mob of pro-southern citizens threw stones at the Yankee troops and shots were fired as four soldiers were killed and twelve civilians lost their lives. The state was divided, the eastern section had close ties to the south, both economic and social, while the western region was more allied to the North. When Federal troops occupied Baltimore, the Federal government managed state affairs and Maryland, though divisive, remained neutral.

John Gill of Baltimore, his younger brother Somerville Pinkney Gill and their cousin George M. Gill, three young sons of Maryland, caught up in the fervor of the times, made their decision to fight in defense of the South. When the four years of the tragic struggle ended, Somerville and George had given their lives for what they believed in. As George breathed his last in the presence of an old mountaineer who had so carefully cared for him, he uttered the last words of a Southern fighting man, "I died at least in a good cause." He was buried on a mountain-side cemetery while Somerville, a month earlier, had been buried in a mass grave by Union troops south of Petersburg, Virginia. John was wounded and nearly died of disease and later, after being paroled, was taken prisoner before, at last, he returned home.

When the guns ceased firing at Appomattox all was lost, but John had the great satisfaction of knowing he had served the Army of Northern Virginia and the Confederacy with distinction. No greater accolade could be given him than the statement of Fitzhugh Lee, nephew of General Robert E. Lee, formerly Major General and Commander of the Cavalry Corps, Army of Northern Virginia and Governor of Virginia from 1885 to 1889. These praiseworthy remarks of this notable Virginian are as follows:

RICHMOND, VA., March 22, 1904.

John Gill, of Baltimore, served at my headquarters and near my side for the greater part of the war from 1861 to 1865. He was one of a number of heroic Marylanders who left their homes to join and do service in behalf of the South.

I had him detailed to report to me because I had been informed that he was a good soldier and performed all the duties confided to him in a satisfactory manner. I first assigned him to duty as a courier, and afterwards promoted him to be Sergeant in the Division Signal Corps. I found him active, vigilant, energetic and courageous in the various encounters between my command and the Federal Cavalry. I am correctly quoted as having stated years ago that I would be glad to lead in a fight 5,000 men like John Gill against 10,000 of the enemy.

He should know what he is writing about, because whenever the opportunity occurred his place in the war picture was near the flashing of the guns.

FITZHUGH LEE,
Formerly Major-General Commanding Cavalry Corps of the Army of Northern Virginia.

FOREWORD

These recently discovered memoirs of John Gill of Baltimore, Maryland, are not known to have been available to the general public. No changes in the narrative have been made. The illustrations, maps, index and bibliography have been added to enhance the story's content.

John Gill's fascinating story of his wartime experiences which include many exciting exploits, as well as tragedies, keeps the reader's interest alive. His words of dedication are those in memory of his brother who gave his life to the cause in which he believed.

MEMOIRS OF JOHN GILL

DEDICATION

Dedicated to the memory of my dear brother, who gave his life to the cause of the South.

He sleeps on the battle-field, but will awaken at the call of the redeemed, and be blessed for evermore.

"There is a bright abode reserved for all good soldiers who die in action."

My grandfather, John Gill, of Alexandria, Virginia, the son of Thomas Gill of Notton, Yorkshire, England, came to this country just after the close of the American Revolution, as the resident partner of the shipping firm of Abernethy, Lowry & Gill, of London, one of the leading firms of that time.

My grandmother Gill was Esther Lowry, daughter of Col. William Lowry and Olivia Pickens, his wife, both from Castle Blaney, County Monaghan, Ireland.

Colonel Lowry came to Baltimore in 1794, and shortly after was commissioned by Governor Lee, of Maryland, Major of the 27th Regiment, Maryland Volunteers. He was subsequently made Colonel of the Regiment.

His son, J. Lowry Donaldson, was Adjutant of the 27th Regiment in the battle of North Point, in which he was killed. He was a distinguished lawyer and a member of the Maryland Legislature. His name was changed by an Act of Assembly from Lowry to Donaldson, in compliance with the request of a rich uncle of that name, residing in London.

My father was Richard W. Gill, son of John Gill, of Alexandria, Virginia. My mother was Ann E. Deale, daughter of Captain James Deale, West River, Anne Arundel County, Md. My great grandfather, Captain John Deale, was an officer in the 31st Weems Battalion, and served during the Revolution in defence of Annapolis and that portion of the county bordering on the Chesapeake Bay. My maternal grandmother was a Franklin, whose family were large property and slave owners in Anne Arundel County.

I was born August 15, 1841, in the City of Annapolis. My father died February 28, 1852, when I was only ten years old.

My mother was left with four children, two girls and two boys. Fortunately my father had left an estate sufficient to provide comfortably for all of us, and my mother, being a woman of most excellent sense and judgment, made the best possible disposition of her income with the view of educating her children.

My father's death left a scar that time could never efface. One of his associates at the bar, in announcing his death to a full bench of the Court of Appeals of Maryland, said: "I will not attempt to eulogize the dead, but I cannot refrain from saying that I have never known one who more deservedly and universally possessed the esteem of all who knew him."

For several years after my father's death we were all kept at home. My mother had secured a most excellent governess, a Miss Boyce, who proved most satisfactory and was liked so much that she soon became part of our household.

At the age of about 15 I was sent to the Preparatory School of St. John's College. In 1856 my mother and sisters concluded that it was best for me to go to a boarding-school, and the Lawrenceville High School, near Princeton, New Jersey, was selected.

I shall never cease being grateful to my dear mother for sending me to this school. At the head of it was a very distinguished educator, Dr. Samuel Hamill, well known throughout the country, and the best man I ever knew to train boys in the way they should go.

I graduated at Lawrenceville during the fall of 1859, and from there went to the University of Virginia.

At the outbreak of the Civil War, 1861, I enlisted as a private soldier in the Confederate Army.

"All things have worked together for my good."

JOHN GILL
Courtesy Sun Printing Co., Baltimore, Md.

Maryland

CHAPTER I

WAR BREAKS OUT ————————————————

It was forty-two years ago last spring since the first mutterings of the Civil War alarmed the country. Already several of the Southern States had withdrawn from the Union, and in the early part of 1861 it was evident that others would soon follow.

As I was born a Marylander, my early education and training pointed in one direction. My family for many years, especially on my mother's side, had owned slaves, and I had never been taught to believe that slavery was a sin or a crime. All my early sympathies and associations were decidedly averse from these opinions.

Therefore, when the question as to the right of these States to separate peaceably from the compact formed by their forefathers was resisted and denied by one section of the country, I was not long in deciding the question for myself. I determined at once which cause to espouse, and to take up arms to defend it. I was a mere boy at the time, scarcely nineteen years of age. Two years before my mother had sent me to the University of Virginia, hoping that my education would some day fit me, in some small degree, to follow in the footsteps of my illustrious father, who, although dead ten years before the outbreak of the war, had left behind him an enviable reputation for high character and distinguished services to his State as a jurist and useful citizen.

While at the University I formed many early attachments, especially among the Southern students, and when the issue arose I felt their destiny to be my destiny. Oh, how bright and happy were the days preceding the war! What pleasant associations still ring out from those old University walls! How little did we know, or how little did we think what a change would soon take place;

what the magnitude of that change would be! Some predicted a short war; the issue would soon be settled in a few months. Others shook their heads and looked aghast at the prospect before them. Well, the war lasted four years, four long, dreary years, years of trials and hardships unequaled in the annals of war.

We were told when we were school-boys that our forefathers in the struggle for American independence, suffered and endured every privation, but when I compare the events of these two epochs, I question very much if their trials were greater than ours; at least I hope not.

The country was now thoroughly aroused. Fort Sumter had been fired upon, and both sides were calling for volunteers. Mr. Lincoln had issued his proclamation for 75,000 troops. The South was not idle. The call to arms was heard throughout the land.

On the part of the North, troops were being rapidly moved forward to Washington to defend the National Capital. The Southerners were concentrating in the vicinity of Richmond, Virginia, to defend that city, which was to become the capital of the new Confederacy.

I had returned to Baltimore, and found great excitement throughout the State. In an effort to pass Northern soldiers through the city, men of Southern sympathy arose and organized to resist. On the 19th of April, 1861, the 6th Massachusetts Regiment, which was marching up Pratt Street from the President Street Station to the B. & O. depot, were fired upon and severely handled by an excited mob. Maryland was now thoroughly aroused and realized that all State rights were ignored by the general government, and if not already she would soon be under bayonet rule.

There was a general call to arms, and troops were sent to the Susquehanna to destroy the bridge over that river. Every obstacle was devised to retard Northern troops reaching Washington. I became a member of the Maryland guard. We were drilled day and night to get ready to fight and resist any further attempt to pass soldiers through the State. While this was going on, a large body of troops was being transported from Havre de Grace by water to Annapolis, and thence by rail to Washington. In this way, in a short time, Maryland had a large hostile army to hold her in subjection, and those of her sons who were still ready to fight for her soon realized that they could fight only by removing the seat of war south of the Potomac River.

I concluded at once to start south. The first thing to do was to go to Annapolis, the place of my birth, my old home, and say good-bye to my mother and sister, who were supposed to be still there. I had had no communication with them for a week or ten days, and took it for granted that they were at home. Imagine my deep regret, therefore, upon arriving at Annapolis, to find that they had left the city on one of the Government transports bound for New London. Many citizens of Annapolis, especially those connected with the army and navy, had availed themselves of this opportunity to remove their families to a place of safety and far away from the seat of war.

My mother and sister had many friends among the officers of the Navy, and it was through the kindness of Captain Joseph Miller that they were cared for in this good manner.

What a crushing blow to me not to see my dear mother! But it has often occurred to me since that it was just as well that we did not meet, as the parting would have been heartbreaking in the extreme. This was about May the 1st, when most of my friends and relatives had fled from the city. I ventured, however, before getting my horse, which had been engaged at a livery stable, to go down to the Academy, to say farewell to some of my old friends and inform them of my intentions, some of whom I should never see again.

I shall never forget that night. Notwithstanding the fact that I was soon to take up arms against the Government, these old friends were friends still, and it was trying to break the cord which had so long united us in friendly and social intercourse.

Midnight was rapidly approaching when I went to the stable, and mounting my horse rode away to South river. On coming to the ferry, the ferryman of course was asleep and no boat was crossing at that hour. However, I soon roused him up, and he knew, without asking me, what I was after and what I was doing. I paid him the ferriage, and said good-bye. I think he would have been delighted to go with me, but we exchanged very few remarks about the war.

I rode on to Cedar Park, the ancestral home of the Mercers. Arriving there early in the morning, some hours before breakfast, I had time to put up my horse and prepare myself a little before being presented to the ladies.

In regard to West river, there are very few people in Maryland today who can recall what West river was before the war. It was a thickly settled agricultural and aristocratic neighborhood, situated between Rhodes and West rivers, forming a peninsula, and the land was owned by some of the most cultivated and attractive people in the State, containing some of the oldest families: the Mercers, Markoes, Hughes, Maxcys, Deales, Contees, Steuarts, Chestons, Murrays, Brogdens, Sellmans, Steeles and Franklins. Some of the estates were extremely well kept, and were the frequent scenes of great social gatherings at certain seasons of the year. Cedar Park was particularly noted for its hospitality and charming daughters.

As before stated, I had arrived early in the morning and was already standing in the hall when first to welcome me appeared the charming hostess of the house, Mrs. Mercer. She was soon followed by her two daughters, Miss Sophie and Miss Mary, together with Miss Jennie Swann, daughter of ex-Governor Swann of Maryland, and Miss Markoe, a sister of the present Colonel Frank Markoe of the 5th Maryland Regiment. And what a welcome it was! They all knew the disturbed condition of the country, and especially the condition of affairs in Baltimore, and insisted at once that I should make my stay at Cedar Park as long as possible. Under the circumstances, this was not hard to do, but it was hard to get away when once fixed there, particularly from such irresistible and charming young women.

Well, at breakfast, when the servants retired from the room (and those were good, old slave days in Maryland when the darkey knew his place, when it was the custom for the servants to retire after the breakfast had been placed upon the table), I soon informed them of my plans, and that in a few days I expected to gather together several young men in the neighborhood and start for the South.

I was not long in securing recruits. Jim McCaleb, Harry Stuart, together with two young men, one by the name of Owens and the other Jones, and myself, formed a party of five. This was about the 5th or 6th of May. We arranged to start on our march the following night. Each of us possessed a good horse and a Colt's revolver. By appointment we all met at our rendezvous, and rode away through Anne Arundel County until we reached the beautiful old home of Doctor Richard Stuart, historically known as Dodan, now the home of a Catholic sisterhood.

Doctor Stuart's family were rebels by inheritance, and there was no attempt to disguise this fact on the part of anyone. We all sat down to a glorious Maryland supper, and only left late in the evening with God's blessing upon our heads. We soon cross-ed the line of Anne Arundel into Prince George's and rode to the home of Captain John Contee, a retired U.S. Naval officer. It was with some difficulty that we rapped the old Captain up at that hour of the night. He, however, put his head out of the window and we invited him down to meet us. He was a thorough Maryland gentleman of the old school, and before making any inquiry as to our plans and movements, he invited us to join him in a glass of whisky and water.

His beautiful daughter, Miss Florence, soon put in an appearance. It was just two o'clock in the morning, and in a few minutes we were again sitting down to a healthful repast of cold meat, cold bread and butter, pickles, whisky, milk, etc.

The Captain had already asked us to take several drinks in the short space of fifteen minutes, and we were all fast getting into a happy frame of mind. When we told the Captain we were going South, he said: "Gentlemen, you know I am a retired naval officer, and having served my country so long, I shall continue to uphold the flag. I would advise you young men to retrace your steps and return to your homes." Miss Florence held opposite views, and she was loud in her exclamations of praise that we were on our way to fight for the South.

I soon found we were tarrying too long, being too hospitably treated. We indulged again in the Captain's good whisky, and when we mounted and said good-bye, we were prepared to oppose anything that came in our way.

The sun was rising on a bright May Sabbath morn as we rode into Laurel, a small village on the line of the Baltimore & Ohio Railroad.

Our itinerary directed us to take the road to Rockville, Montgomery County, but just outside of Laurel, and after having crossed the railroad track, we were met by a man driving a wagon, who informed us that a Yankee regiment had just encamped at Rockville about eight miles away, and that if it was our intention to pass through that town we had better scatter. It was very evident that we could not keep together, and after a short conference we decided that two would take the open country to the left, two the open country to the right, and that I should continue on the main road, going through the town, as originally designed, and join the others that evening at Claggett's Ford.

Just as I was entering the town of Rockville, I fancied I would escape the notice of the troops, but I had scarcely moved a step further when I saw several officers sitting on the fence on both sides of the road. There was nothing to do but to ride straight on. I passed through them and bowed graciously, when one of the officers cried, "Will you sell that horse?" I was quite equal to the occasion, and replied, "Yes, I will on my return. I am on my way to pay a visit to Major Peters, who lives a few miles up the road. I expect to come back this way Wednesday, and will sell you the horse if you will give me $250 for him." Of course, I changed my mind and never came back. A fib, under such circumstances, was excusable.

I was not further molested, and after riding a couple of miles I reached Claggett's house, and from there was directed to Claggett's Ford. I was surprised to find my comrades already there, and as it was getting quite dark we arranged to spend the night in the culvert under the Chesapeake & Ohio canal.

It was through this culvert that we were to reach the river in the morning, an unfrequented route across the Potomac. We had been advised that it was but seldom used.

We realized that we should have to sleep either on the banks of the river that night or under the culvert, when suddenly, to our great surprise, we heard a cry of a sentinel on the towpath "All's well". This went through us like a shot; it necessitated absolute silence on our part; so that we were obliged to stand by our horses' heads to prevent them from neighing.

It was a long and tiresome night, especially for young men who had had so little experience in such matters. The day was breaking when a question arose in our minds what to do with the sentinel. We must either shoot or capture him to avoid a general alarm before we crossed over the river. This question had to be decided at once, as the day was breaking rapidly. We made Jim McCaleb our Captain, and he, being a resolute chap, ordered Harry Stuart to creep up the canal bank, with orders either to capture or kill the sentinel.

We waited some time in dread suspense, expecting every minute to hear the crack of Stuart's revolver, but not a sound was heard. Stuart finally crawled back into the culvert and said, "The pickets that we heard during the night have all been called in." Evidently they were on duty at night but relieved during the day. We were all very thankful to have matters take this shape, and no one was hurt. We should have deeply regretted taking the life of a soldier or picket under such circumstances.

There was no time to be lost. We were at once in the saddle, on the river's bank, into the water, plunging and swimming through rocks and holes, pressing on to the Virginia side.

In a few minutes more we safely landed. We got breakfast at a farmer's house, and afterwards he directed us on the road to Leesburg. We were wet to the skin. Without waiting to dry our clothes, and having no change with us, we pushed on.

On our arrival rooms were engaged at Pickett's hotel, and our horses were stabled for the night. We had fires made in our rooms and dried our clothes. In a short while we were in presentable shape.

We went out to see the sights and talk to the people. No introduction was needed. The fact that we were Marylanders and had come over to fight for Virginia gave us a hearty and hospitable welcome from all the citizens.

Leesburg was always noted for her pretty women, and we had a very pleasant evening with a great many of them. We were the recipients of much hospitality. Unfortunately the next day I fell sick, just as sick as I could be. I had evidently caught cold crossing the river, together with exposure to the heat, drinking and eating imprudently, doing everything in fact I ought not to have done, which resulted in a violent attack of dysentery. The country doctor was called in, and I was ordered immediately to bed to remain there until told by him to get up.

That very night, about midnight, cries were heard in the streets, people rushing to and fro and great excitement prevailing everywhere. The report had come into the town that the Yankees had crossed the Potomac at Edwards's Ferry in large force, and that a company of Maryland cavalry, commanded by Captain Gaither, then picketed at that point, were being rapidly driven in, and were retreating on the town. This, of course, started a panic in Leesburg. The houses were deserted, the hotel abandoned, the stables emptied, and no one remained with me but my faithful friend McCaleb, who declared he would not desert me no matter what happened.

He came into my room and sat down by my side, both of us momentarily expecting the Yankees to enter the room. Hour after hour we waited without closing our eyes.

It proved a false alarm. The next morning I said to McCaleb: "Jim, I think with a little breakfast, I should feel better, and perhaps later in the day we could start on our way to join Ashby's cavalry. Go down stairs, old fellow, and see if our horses have been fed, and send me up some breakfast." McCaleb was not long gone. I could see by his expression that there was something to worry him more than Yankees. Almost breathless, he exclaimed, "Our horses have been stolen; there is no food in the kitchen and nothing for breakfast." I really felt like giving up the ghost, to lose that splendid horse of mine, for which I had so recently given $250 in gold, which money I had been a long time accumulating. It was enough to break a young cavalier's heart, to see his ambition shattered in this way. This noble charger was stolen from the stable that night by some comrade or Confederate, and I have never, from that day to this, found a trace of him. All my plans and hopes to join Ashby's command were at an end. As I had no money excepting a few dollars left in my pocket and was weak and sick, McCaleb and I were sorely perplexed to determine what was next best to do; our disappointment was so keen that we almost cried. We knew that we should make cavalry soldiers, because we had been accustomed from our early youth to ride all kinds of horses, and we felt that under Ashby we should soon make records for ourselves.

But, as already stated, we were nearly out of money, had no one to vouch for us in any way, and there was nothing left to do but to buy a ticket to Richmond, and join the Maryland Infantry then organizing at that point.

CHAPTER II

THE FIRST MARYLAND CONFEDERATE INFANTRY REGIMENT————

We had to take a rather circuitous route in those days to reach Richmond,—by stage from Leesburg to Warrenton, a distance of forty miles, and by rail from Warrenton to Richmond.

On our arrival at Richmond, we put up at the Spottswood Hotel. Here I found a large number of Marylanders as undecided as ourselves as to what command they would join.

Captain William H. Murray, formerly connected with the Maryland Guard in Baltimore, was at Camp Lee recruiting. This company was being made up entirely of Marylanders. Captain Murray was eminently qualified to command the company. He was a good tactician, had been connected with the Guard in Baltimore for some years, and with the material he would gather around him there was no question but that he would organize a notable command.

I must not forget to say that my dear friend McCaleb left me at this time, and we never met again. He went to the far South to visit relatives, afterwards joined the Texas army, and was shot in one of the Trans-Mississippi battles.

There was nothing left for me to do but to join Murray's Company, which I did, and was duly enlisted into the Confederate service on May 17, 1861, to serve one year. We had daily drills and exercises until the Company was fully organized.

We were then ordered to Winchester, Va., to meet other Maryland companies, forming at different points to make up the First Maryland Confederate Regiment. Col. Arnold Elzey, of the old army, was with us at Camp Lee, and it was understood that he should command the regiment then organizing.

Captain George H. Steuart, a gallant son of Maryland, a graduate of West Point as well as a young officer who had seen considerable service in fighting the Indians, was to be our Lieut.-Colonel. Bradley T. Johnson, of Frederick, a young lawyer, was to be the Major. Probably there was no regiment in the service that started out under brighter auspices or with better officers than the First Maryland.

The different companies came together at Winchester and were mustered into service to serve for twelve months. It made very little difference to the men who were to command them, provided the officers were all Marylanders.

We can all say with much pride that Elzey, Steuart and Johnson maintained throughout the war the highest distinction for bravery and soldierly conduct. Elzey and Steuart rose to be Major-Generals, and Johnson, although only a civilian, soon rose with distinction to the rank of Brigadier-General. His military career was phenomenal, and to have had Lee, Joe Johnston and Jackson compliment him on the field was no small honor; he was recognized as a soldier most gallant and distinguished in the service of the South.

The 1st Maryland was put into a brigade composed of the 3d Tennessee, the 13th Virginia and the 10th Virginia, under command of General Kirby Smith.

General Patterson, commanding the Federal forces, was organizing an army in the vicinity of Hagerstown, and was reported to have crossed the Potomac near Falling Waters, and to be marching toward Bunker Hill to engage our little army.

Col. Jackson, afterwards known as "Stonewall," was sent forward to reconnoitre and report Patterson's position. Jackson simply felt the enemy, capturing only a few prisoners, and no decisive engagement took place. He accomplished, however, the object of his mission, which gave General Johnston an insight into Patterson's whereabouts, and no doubt other valuable information in regard to the strength of his army.

We had already moved up ten miles north of Winchester to a small village named Darkesville. Here we celebrated the 4th of July, '61. We were drawn up in line of battle, expecting Patterson to come out and give us fight.

CAPT. WILLIAM H. MURRAY
1ST MARYLAND BATTALION,
C.S.A.
Courtesy Time Life Books

It was on this day that I remember having received the first letters from home, one from my dear mother and another from my aunt. My mother's letter was terribly sad, a message from a heart-broken woman. My aunt, who had bitterly opposed my going South and taking up arms against the Union, was not long in changing her views and her opinion of the question before the country. In her letter to me she said, "My nephew, I honor you for your self-sacrifice."

General Johnston rode down the line of battle on the Fourth of July, and stopping in front of our regiment said to Col. Elzey, "If your men fight as well as they yell, I expect good sevice of them." We remained in line of battle for several days, but each day Patterson declined to fight. It was hard and most depressing to stand out in the broiling sun without shelter of any kind, waiting for a clash with the enemy. We held a good position and were anxious to have Patterson attack us.

General Patterson displayed more military ability than we had given him credit for. Instead of attacking us in front, he made a detour to the left, and tried to outflank us. Johnston was on the alert and fell back toward Winchester, again taking up his original position, which was stronger and nearer our base of supplies.

We were kept busy in throwing up breastworks and mounting heavy guns, which was all good training, besides picketing on the outposts.

These experiences were rapidly forming us into good, raw troops and preparing us for the great conflict so near at hand, but which we little dreamed of.

On the 17th of July orders were received to break camp and prepare to march. As is the case with all raw troops, they think they know as much as their commanders, and if orders don't suit them, they are not inclined to obey them. There was quite a disposition to mutiny throughout the army when the different regiments moved into the turnpike, to find that the order was to

PVT. JOHN HAYDEN
1ST MARYLAND BATTALION,
C.S.A.
Courtesy Time Life Books

march to the right instead of to the left. To march to the right was to march away from the enemy, and at the moment it looked like a further retreat.

We were not long in suspense. A general order was read to the army that General Beauregard, at Manassas, was threatened by an overwhelming force of the enemy under General McDowell, and we were marching to his support, and every soldier was instructed to step out. This settled the question at once. I never saw men march before or since the war with such alacrity. Every soldier was in his place; not a laggard in the line. So we pressed on to the Shenandoah, marching all night long and reaching the river at early dawn.

We went into the river, up to our necks, with our guns and ammunition raised over our heads, and the current was so swift that some of us locked arms to support each other. I remember that Southgate Lemmon and Tom Levering, my comrades, helped me across the river, and their assistance was very needful, otherwise I might have gone down. The march continued with wet clothes through Upperville to Piedmont Station, on the Manassas Gap Railroad. We encamped along the line of the road late Saturday night, July 20th, 1861.

McDowell's army at Centreville, moving on Manassas, took position for the battle the following day. We were all eager for a fight. Every man was in position, and all orders were cheerfully obeyed. We slept a little that night, but before 3 A.M. Sunday we were up and crowding into cars for a trip to the plains of Manassas. Our regiment, in fact our brigade, was the last to leave.

The fight had already begun. We could hear the cannon roar. The train which conveyed us stopped within three miles of Manassas Junction, about 1 o'clock on that hot Sabbath day.

The line was immediately formed, and a rapid march began in a northwesterly direction, to be in touch with the extreme left of our line. The heat was intense. Through ploughed fields and dusty roads we marched. No doubt the enemy was made aware of our coming in this way. As we came near the order was given to "double quick."

General Smith said: "Boys, if you double quick, you will still have a chance to get in the fight." We knew that we were nearing the battle-field, as the dead and wounded could be seen and heard on each side of us. Many said we were whipped; others said, "Go in boys, give them hell."

The arrival of Kirby Smith's brigade was most timely. Jackson had been wounded. Bee and Bartow fighting at the head of their regiments against desperate odds, had fallen dead at their posts. General Smith repeated the command "Step lively, boys, and we will be in time yet for a fight." So on we swept, cheer after cheer, marching with the thermometer at nearly 105, no water, tongues parched with red clay, when we came to a little stream where horses had fallen dead during the day; the water was already colored with blood, but we sipped it up as a refreshing beverage.

We were moved up rapidly. It was just at this point that the first bullet from the enemy shot a member of Company C, John Berryman. The shot was fired from a regiment of Brooklyn Zouaves, that, under cover, fired a volley into us, wounding several men, but, comparatively speaking, doing but little damage. We here formed into line and returned this fire, driving the enemy from cover. General Smith was in the act of forming his brigade into line of battle when he was shot and fell from his horse. This was the first real live soldier that I had seen shot and fall from a horse, and of course I thought he was dead. He lived, however, to achieve an enviable reputation as a soldier, as well as a distinguished citizen and educator of the young men of the South.

Col. Elzey, the senior Colonel, took command of the brigade. We moved on, steadily feeling the enemy in our front. We were ordered to lie down for a moment, until the artillery, under Lieut. Beckham, could take position on our left.

The artillery, concealed in the woods, opened a rapid and effective fire, creating havoc and confusion, when the order came for us to fix bayonets and charge. The enemy's line of battle, the extreme right of the Federal army, held quite a good position, well placed on the crest of a hill. We could see the color-bearer waving the star-spangled banner, and the enemy apparently eager for a fight. Then the order came again to us to charge, and charge we did, straight up the hill in the face of the enemy. It surprised me very much that those fellows should have fired over our heads and wounded so few of us. In a moment more we had broken their lines and captured many prisoners.

The color-bearer just referred to, poor fellow, was shot, and as we passed over his body we saw that he had entwined himself in the American flag. Our men, one and all, had a kind word for the gallant soldier. I think he came from the State of Maine. His regiment, in my opinion could have stayed there a little longer. Changing our front obliquely to the right, we could see the enemy in full retreat. There is no question but that the timely arrival of Kirby Smith's brigade had a most important influence in determining the result of that day, and General Smith goes down in history as the Blucher.

It was getting late in the afternoon, and no orders to pursue the enemy had been received. Colonel Elzey moved a portion of the brigade, including our regiment, to a point where the fight had been hottest, and where we saw two regular batteries of artillery completely annihilated, horses and men lying piled up dead and no one left but an old cannoneer, still standing by his gun ready to load. It was just at this point that Beauregard rode up and promoted Elzey on the field to be a Brigadier-General. I have participated in and seen a great many battles since that fight, especially Cold Harbor, Gettysburg, Spottsylvania, and I might mention others, but for a short distance along the line, the slaughter of the enemy was as appalling as anything I witnessed during the war.

The fighting had been terrific in front of Jackson, and down Bee's and Bartow's lines. The contending forces along this position had, on several occasions during the day, crossed bayonets. McHenry Howard and I tried to do something to alleviate the sufferings of the wounded. I remember offering my canteen to some of the poor Federals and was surprised to find that their minds were so poisoned against Southerners as to think we desired to give them poison to drink. It was necessary to drink the water from the canteen first myself before I could restore confidence in these dying men, and they gasped, "Thank God, thank God!"

We went into camp several miles from the stone bridge. It had been a hard and rough day. We had had nothing to eat, and no rations were issued until noon of the next day; but we all sank down to rest that night with thankful hearts that death had not come to us.

It was our first battle, and although our regiment had not been hotly engaged at any time, still its behavior had been such as to establish a mutual confidence of man to man that the right stuff was there, and we should be heard from whenever the occasion required.

From this time until the following spring there were no battles fought; it was mere routine camp duty with occasional skirmishes on the picket-line. I shall not attempt to describe the experiences of camp life and other events incident to the life of a private soldier during this period.

CHAPTER III

TYPHOID FEVER ─────────────────

The early autumn of 1861 was spent in the vicinity of Fairfax C.H. With no enemy near, many of the soldiers were permitted to visit the farmers' and officers' houses, and in this way we formed very pleasant acquaintances and associations. The life, however, was saddened by the sanitary condition of the army. In fact, the whole army was infected with all manner of diseases—fever, measles, whooping-cough, but particularly typhoid fever.

I think it was in the early part of September that I was stricken down with typhoid fever. I was ill for more than nine weeks. Most of the time I lay on the hard ground, receiving very little attention from anybody. My life was almost despaired of, and no doubt I should have died but for a providential occurrence.

I asked my doctor one morning what were my chances of recovery, and his reply was not cheerful. I said to him, "Doctor, if you will only take me to a house, strip me of these vile clothes filled with vermin and put me in a clean bed, I shall live." The Lord was truly merciful to me, for on the very day of this conversation a messenger, as it were, arrived in the form of a gentleman from Fauquier County, Virginia, who came in his carriage to take a few of the sick soldiers to his home.

He said he had come specially to look after the sick Marylanders, who had no homes in his country, and the Doctor and officers of my company singled me out as one of the sickest in the camp. I was put on a couch and carried by four faithful comrades to the station, and from there conveyed in an open freight car some thirty miles to Piedmont Station on the Manassas Gap Railroad.

I reached there late in the afternoon to find an ox-cart with a mattress in the bottom, to carry me to Bollingbrook, the beautiful estate of Mr. Robert Bolling, of Fauquier County, Va. The old ox-cart, although it had a mattress, gave me a good jolting, as may be imagined, before arriving at his house.

In fact, I may say I was nearly dead when I got there. The good servants carried me in their arms to a room on the second floor. Here they stripped off the old clothes from my body, and with hot water and alcohol bathed my bed sores. I was almost a Lazarus. A nice clean night-shirt was put on, and a glass of old Port revived my waning spirits, and just before the tea-bell rang I found myself in a comfortable bed surrounded by genuine Virginia hospitality, and refined, sympathetic people who were ready to make every sacrifice for my comfort. I fell asleep that night without my usual dose of morphia, and it was a sweet sleep, for during the night the fever left me, and I awoke in the morning feeling that a change had come over me.

By careful nursing, day by day, I gradually grew better. The beautiful Miss Tabb Bolling, of Petersburg, Va., afterwards Mrs. Gen. Wm. F. H. Lee, and her cousin, Miss Anna Bolling, of Bollingbrook, were in constant attendance, and they did as much for me as a sister would do for a brother.

In the course of three weeks I was permitted to sit up, and a few days later I was taken down stairs for a comfortable seat on the porch. I was gaining strength rapidly, and looked forward to meeting my old comrades again in a few weeks.

Let me stop here to say a word. The men from Maryland, away from their homes, especially those who were sick (and most of them took their turn at it) owe an everlasting debt of gratitude to the women of Virginia. And what can we say about them? What splendid women they were! What self-sacrifices they endured, and with what heroism and courage they withstood the horrors of those terrible times!

I would mention here a long list of names of families kind to me during the war, but let a few suffice. The Bollings, McFarlands, Braxtons, Alexanders, Stephensons, Pendletons, Buchanans, Dandridges, and Washingtons were only a few of the noble families to whom I owe a lasting gratitude, and whom I hope never to forget.

I remained at Bollingbrook until late in November and then bade adieu to those charming surroundings, to return to my regiment encamped at Manassas Junction. How pleasant it was to see the faces of my old comrades again! There was Gres Hough, Nick Watkins, Sam Sindall, Frank Markoe, South Lemmon and others, whose names at the moment I cannot recall. They all greeted me most affectionately.

They had built a very comfortable log hut for the winter, and were living the lives of real soldiers. I was soon at home and initiated into the mysteries of camp life once more. Several hours each day were devoted to camp exercises and drill, hunting wild turkeys, playing cards, and on Sunday some clergyman would come in and preach to the camp.

I vividly recall Bishop Johns, of Virginia. He was interested in all the young men, and particularly in those from Maryland, and the men of the regiment were always glad to see him and listen to the gospel story as told by him.

Here in winter quarters we were working hard preparing for the opening of the spring campaign of 1862.

CHAPTER IV

WITH JACKSON IN THE VALLEY ─────────

We broke camp at Manassas early in March, 1862, and retired to the Rappahannock River. Our brigade became now a part of Ewell's Division, Jackson's Corps, Army of Northern Virginia. The main army, under command of Gen. Joseph E. Johnston, continued its march towards Gordonsville, while our division remained on the Rappahannock.

The weather was simply wretched, so much so that it was most difficult, in fact next to an impossibility, for the army to move. Here we remained about six weeks, when finally we received orders to cross the Blue Ridge and report to General Jackson in the Valley. General Jackson had about this time encountered the enemy at Kernstown, and while compelled to retire, he had made one of the most gallant fights of the war, overwhelmed as he was by superior numbers.

Our Division halted at Conrad's Store in the Luray Valley. To our great surprise, Jackson had gone when we arrived. The old story is that Ewell sat on the fence and cried because no one could tell him of Jackson's wherabouts. We could get no tidings of Jackson; no one knew where to find him; his camp had been abandoned, and all that was known was that he had moved rapidly in the direction of Staunton, Va.

Jackson had his plans, however, and was preparing to make another of his brilliant maneuvers. A large Federal force under General Milroy was advancing towards McDowell in what is now West Virginia. This was a portion of Fremont's army, and Jackson, to carry out his plan of defeating Banks, at Winchester, must first destroy Milroy in Virginia. This movement was a success. He made a very rapid march, met the enemy and accomplished his purpose, retraced his steps as rapidly as possible and rejoined Gen. Ewell.

A part of Jackson's plan was to destroy Banks at Winchester, and carry out President Davis's and Gen. Johnston's scheme,—even if it involved the withdrawal of a large body of troops from the peninsula,—and reach the North by way of the Valley, striking a sudden and heavy blow at some exposed position, capturing Washington if possible.

These plans, however, never fully materialized. After the battle of McDowell, where the enemy had been repulsed at every point, and Jackson had driven them sufficiently to the rear to cover his own movement, he pressed on down the Valley.

General Banks retired as rapidly as possible to Winchester, where the principal engagement of the campaign took place, resulting ultimately in a complete overthrow of the occupation of the Valley of Virginia by Northern troops.

General Ewell moved from Conrad's Store to Front Royal, and Jackson from Harrisonburg to the same place. This movement began on May 18, 1862. As Ewell's Division approached Front Royal, General Ewell was informed by the citizens that Col. Kenly, a Marylander, commanding about 1,000 Marylanders, with a battery of artillery, was in command at that point.

Our regiment that morning was bringing up the rear of Ewell's Division, when Gen. Ewell transmitted an order to Bradley T. Johnson, that it had been reported to him that the enemy in his front were Marylanders, and if we wished to meet Marylanders, to move our regiment to the front at once.

The challenge was accepted immediately, and the whole army halted that we might take the front skirmish line, which position we held throughout the fight, and finally routed the enemy, our fellow citizens from Maryland.

I forgot to mention that about this time the first year's service of the Maryland regiment had expired, and the men were entitled to an honorable discharge with privilege of re-enlisting, or entering other branches of the service.

We were mustered out on the 17th day of May in accordance with law, but to the credit of the men be it stated that every man took his old place in the ranks, to participate in the glorious succession of victories which were to crown Jackson's campaign.

The first fight took place at Front Royal, the 1st Maryland leading the advance of Ewell's Division. Colonel Kenly made a good fight and displayed conspicuous gallantry in the field, but he was over-matched. His conduct was the admiration of every soldier. He was captured with more than 600 prisoners. The last stand was made at the bridge over the Shenandoah River, and I distinctly recall one poor fellow who fell dead just as he turned to cross the bridge. He was in my immediate front. We were double-quicking and firing at the same time. I am not positive who killed him; I am glad I am not able to say; bullets were flying thick and fast. He was a well-dressed officer, and as I came up to his dead body I could not resist relieving him of a long pair of cavalry boots which he wore. The temptation was too great and I could not let some one else make this important capture. I stooped down and relieved him of them, and found them to be of great service for months and months after, and especially when I joined the cavalry a few weeks later.

Jackson and Ewell pressed on to Winchester. We were getting a good taste of Jackson's foot cavalry at that time, marching from 20 to 30 miles a day, and frequently without food of any kind.

As is usual after typhoid fever, one grows fat; my weight reached 180 pounds, but after the Valley campaign, and marching some five or six hundred miles in forty days, I settled down to 136 pounds. I was never in better health or better fighting trim in my life.

Just before the battle of Winchester, Jackson called on Ewell for our brigade. We were placed under Jackson's immediate command on the extreme left. The other two brigades of Ewell's Division had gone into action on the right.

We were held in reserve until the battle was well under way, when Elzey moved, left in rear, to turn, if possible, the enemy's right.

General Gordon, of the Federal army, was in immediate command of Bank's forces in our front, and he must have been a soldier of some skill as he anticipated this movement and prevented the success which we had hoped for. They fired upon us at close range, but it did not check our advance.

Then it was that Dick Taylor, commanding the gallant Louisianians, rose suddenly from cover just to our right and the two brigades swept irresistibly forward, the Yankees giving way at every point. Jackson urged his men to press on to the Potomac, and our brigade led in the pursuit. The Northern troops were falling in every direction. The fruits of this victory, however, were lost, excepting the enormous supplies captured in Winchester, owing to the lack of disciplined cavalry. If Jackson had had cavalry, the entire army of Banks would have been captured before they reached the Potomac River. After the battle one almost seemed compensated for risking his life, especially on an occasion like the taking of Winchester, to see the people hail us as their deliverers. They were almost frantic with joy, and it is said that General Jackson smiled and asked a lady, "Who's been here since I've been gone?"

We were all too tired to push the enemy and therefore they escaped to the Potomac. Next morning, however, we continued to march to Halltown, on the direct road to Harper's Ferry.

The afternoon of the day following we stormed Bolivar Heights, Gen. George H. Steuart being in command. This stronghold was held by a Yankee regiment, who were just sitting down to a sumptuous repast when we drove in their pickets, creating such confusion that the tables were all left spread with the supper untouched, so that we could sit down to finish it ourselves.

That regiment could have made a gallant defense, but for some reason they "skedaddled" at the sight of a rebel. We heartily enjoyed their supper. We captured a great many guns and much ammunition without the loss of a single man. That night we slept on the roadside with our faces towards Winchester.

The order came before daybreak to march. We marched the entire day, through Winchester and Middletown on the road to Strasburg up to 10 o'clock that night, covering a distance of 35 miles, and when we rested, we rested without food and with fence-rails for our pillows.

Fortunately the wagons came up in the night and rations were issued at 5 o'clock the following morning. We were soon again on the march, en route for Strasburg. We poor privates knew very little of the danger that surrounded us. We afterwards learned that it was just touch and go whether or not the enemy had entrapped Jackson.

Shields had crossed the Blue Ridge Mountain on the east, and marched from Front Royal towards Strasburg. Fremont was coming on from the west towards Wardensville on our right, and Banks, having learned of our retrograde movement, had recrossed the

Potomac, and, as he supposed, in conjunction with Shields, Milroy and Fremont, Jackson would be gobbled up, but the plan failed for lack of co-operation, and nobody knew better than Jackson how to take advantage of it.

In another day our army was safe; the combined forces of the Federal army were in our rear. We had marched 170 miles in eleven days, and engaged in two battles, Front Royal and Winchester, threatened on all sides by an army of 60,000 against 15,000 under Jackson. We whipped the enemy in detail, and triumphantly escaped from them without losing a single wagon.

Jackson moved slowly up the Valley. His men were tired; they needed rest and food; but he was eternally vigilant awaiting an opportunity to fight. Quite a little skirmish occurred on June 6th, a few miles east of Harrisonburg. General Fremont had sent Percy Wyndham, with a large force of infantry and cavalry, to harass our rear. They met Colonel Turner Ashby, supported by the 58th Virginia Regiment. Ashby had been sent out to check any further advance. A severe fight ensued. Our line wavered, and Ashby, appealing to his men to charge, fell pierced through the heart, and in a moment everything was in confusion.

It was just then that the 1st Maryland, under Col. Bradley T. Johnson, came up in time to save the day. Col. Johnson gave the order to charge, and it was a charge that those who participated in it will never forget. Johnson led us to victory. We were close to the fire of the enemy, it being quite late in the evening, but this did not deter us. On went our regiment until it had routed the crack Pennsylvania Bucktails, capturing 287 prisoners, including Colonel Kane, their commander. We avenged the death of Ashby. This was really the first good fight of our regiment.

We saw many of our comrades fall, but the conduct of the men was simply superb, and General Ewell ordered that we should wear on our colors one of the captured "bucktails" as a trophy.

The next day Gen. Ewell issued a general order, saying that it was due to the intrepid conduct of the 1st Maryland Regiment that the death of Ashby had been avenged. I shall never forget that night: it was one of the saddest of the war. My friend Sam Sindall had been shot while resting his head on my knee just before we were ordered to charge.

Two days later we fought the battle of Cross Keys. Our company were deployed as skirmishers. I was on the advance line for more than six hours, constantly under fire.

We had issued to us 128 rounds of ammunition, and when the fighting in the evening ended we had scarcely a cartridge left. We witnessed the fall of several of our best young men. McKenny White and Willie Colston were desperately wounded, and at the time there seemed little hope for their recovery, but they both survived, the latter meeting a soldier's death at a later period.

Gen. George H. Steuart received a grape shot in the shoulder, which disabled him for nearly six months. I received a slight scratch on the right cheek from a glancing ball, which practically paralyzed my face for some weeks. The next day my cheek was perfectly black. I was struck just as I turned to pick up Lieut. Bean, of Company I, who had been standing immediately in my rear and was wounded in the foot. I had advised him the moment before to get away as he would certainly be struck, but he was a gallant fellow, and did not heed the warning.

I suffered from considerable nausea, produced by this nervous shock, which continued the following day, and I was excused by my Captain from marching with the company; on this account I was not engaged in the battle of Port Republic.

This was the last infantry fight in which I should have taken part. The next day our company went out of service, many of them receiving staff appointments, some re-enlisting in the 2d Maryland Infantry, while others, like myself, joined the cavalry.

I had served more than a year in the infantry.

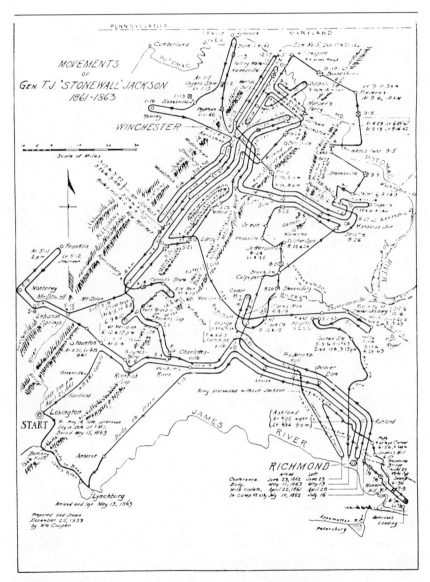

MAP SHOWING ALL OF STONEWALL JACKSON'S MOVEMENTS
Compliments of The Shenandoah Valley Civil War Roundtable

CHAPTER V

COURIER FOR "STONEWALL" JACKSON ———

After the discharge from Murray's Company, we marched with the army to Gordonsville, and there I joined Company A, Maryland Cavalry, Captain Ridgely Brown in command, First Lieutenant Frank A. Bond, Second Lieutenant Thomas Griffith, Third Lieutenant Ventris Pue.

I secured a few days leave of absence, and went by train to Staunton to buy a horse. Succeeding in this, I returned at once to Gordonsville. It would have been difficult indeed to have found a better cavalry organization than the one commanded by Captain Brown.

The company was composed chiefly of men who had been in the infantry for a year, while quite a number of them had recently crossed the Potomac to espouse the cause of the South.

We were temporarily attached to the Second Virginia Cavalry, under Col. Thomas Munford, a gallant and distinguished Virginian, who was particularly proud of his Maryland company, so much so that he placed us as the first company on the right.

Here at Gordonsville General Jackson and his army were resting after the fatiguing Valley campaign. I was in camp, in the woods near General Jackson's headquarters, and while sitting on the fence one evening Captain Pendleton, of Jackson's staff, saw me and inquired if I should like to be detailed for courier duty. We had been old friends at the University of Virginia before the war, and Pendleton said: "Come over to Jackson's headquarters and report for courier duty." With the consent of my Captain, I soon got ready.

General Jackson and staff were lodged in a large white farm-house, with a wooden porch in front, just outside of Gordonsville, and as I rode up I recognized the General walking up and down the porch.

I told him that I had come to report to him for duty as a courier by order of Captain Pendleton, and was ready to receive any orders he might give me. I had never spoken to General Jackson before, although I had frequently seen him on the march and in the Valley.

General Jackson's first order directed me to go to each Brigade headquarters and deliver to each commanding officer positive in-structions to move their respective commands that evening not later than 9 o'clock on the road to Louisa C.H., and when in line to await further orders.

I got back to headquarters about 10 o'clock. I had had some ten brigade commanders to interview, which was no easy task for a green courier like myself. I accomplished the work, however, and reported to General Jackson that the army was moving in ac-cordance with his instructions. He turned to me and asked if I had had anything to eat. I answered that I had not, when he said, "Go down stairs in the dining-room of this house, and you will find my mess-chest. Get something out of it, and report to me at 5 o'clock in the morning."

I enjoyed a hearty supper, and after feeding my horse, fell asleep on the porch, but was aroused in time to be in the saddle at the hour designated.

From that time on, until after the great battles around Rich-mond, I was constantly in the saddle at the great General's side, and I feel that I at least rendered service quite equal, if not fully equal, to that of some of the members of his staff. I was with him on the march from Gordonsville to Louisa C.H., from Louisa C.H. to Hanover Junction, from Hanover Junction to Ashland, from Ashland on the road leading to Pole Green Church, endeavoring to form a line in touch with Hill's Division, then about attacking the enemy at Mechanicsville.

Jackson's corps bore constantly to the left, turning Beaver Dam Creek, moving *en echelon* towards old Cold Harbor.

It was at the beginning of this engagement that I saw Jackson raise his hands to Heaven and pray for victory. Jackson hoped to strike the enemy in rear, and in conjunction with Hill, press him down the Chickahominy. Some confusion and delay prevented the success of this movement, and General Jackson has been criticised for undue delay in taking his proper position, but this question I shall not discuss, because I know he had almost insurmountable obstacles to overcome.

Jackson moved the next morning towards old Cold Harbor, supported by D.H. Hill's Division on his right and Stuart's Cavalry on his left. It was not until quite late in the afternoon, however, that Jackson, hearing the battle raging along Longstreet's and Hill's front, pressed in and hotly engaged the enemy.

Never before nor since have I witnessed such a scene. How I escaped being shot is still a mystery to me, and how my horse escaped is a still greater wonder. Jackson had me constantly "on the go," carrying orders in every direction under fire along the entire line in which Hill's and Ewell's Divisions were engaged.

The fight continued into dark night, and the greatest confusion ensued. I heard someone say the following morning that Jackson and all of his staff had barely escaped capture.

When it was quite dark, we encountered the enemy's outpost in front of us, and Jackson made us charge and capture the post of about twenty men.

We moved early the next morning towards Gaines's Mill, but owing to the destruction of a bridge, we were unable to arrive in time on that day to engage the enemy. Likewise, at the battle of Frazier's farm, we were prevented by the same reason.

I had now been under fire almost constantly for five days. The battle of Frazier's farm occurred on the sixth day. The next morning I was more than gratified to see Colonel Munford, the Colonel of my regiment, report for duty to General Jackson. They had just arrived from the Valley to rejoin the army.

I asked Captain Pendleton to permit me to return to my Company, if my services were no longer needed. The request was granted, and thus I escaped the great and terrible clash of arms which took place the next morning at Malvern Hill.

I had had enough of it for a time at least. Things did not look very pleasant for me around headquarters. General Jackson had been in a bad humor for several days; the truth of the matter is that he and his men had been completely worn out by what they had gone through.

In this battle the Confederates lost 20,000 men; Jackson's Corps almost half that number, and no wonder he was troubled and mortified that, after so great a sacrifice, the enemy had escaped.

CONFEDERATE VIDETTE

GEN. THOMAS "STONEWALL" JACKSON, C.S.A.
Courtesy Valentine Museum

CHAPTER VI

"DRAW SABRES, CHARGE"————————————

The past year had been an extremely eventful period in my life. It was a good thing to be thrown back on one's own resources. I began to grow serious. How I escaped being killed or wounded during the recent terrific campaign has always been a wonder to me. I owe my life to a merciful Providence.

I ascribe a great deal of my success in after life to the hardships and privations endured during the Civil War. Hardships set the mind free to discover, invent and plan.

I professed my faith in God early in life, but I have never felt as though I were a good man, free from shortcomings and frivolities. After all the miraculous escapes during the war, every soldier should try to love God, and try to be the kind of man God would have him to be. I remember distinctly that I soliloquized upon all this just after those terrible seven days' battles around Richmond. They set me to thinking; I was a much better soldier after that experience.

There was great rejoicing in Richmond and throughout the South after the defeat of McClellan, and after the safety of the Capital had been assured.

Our regiment, the Second Virginia Cavalry, did not tarry near Richmond long. We were ordered to join Jackson's forces, a portion of which had already arrived at Gordonsville. This was just preceding the battle of Cedar Mountain.

I cannot recall all that occurred in the early part of this campaign. I did not actively participate in this battle beyond the usual picket and flank duty. I knew that Jackson was preparing to force Pope's army across the Rappahannock, and no doubt there would be another great battle fought when General Lee came up with his main army.

The cavalry, under Jeb Stuart, was harassing Pope's right flank. At midnight, one dark, stormy night, we captured Pope's headquarters at Catlett's Station. This was a great ride. The streams were overflowing their banks. We approached the station from the direction of Warrenton while it was raining hard, and the men were drenched to the skin. It was just the weather for such sport. We swam two streams and reached the coveted spot about midnight.

The camp was surprised by a dashing charge, and the entire command, numbering about 300 prisoners, captured.

We were very much amused the next morning to see one of the men attired in General Pope's full-dress uniform. Pope himself escaped only because he happened to be away that night.

I have a very indistinct recollection of what occurred the following day. I know, however, that we were moving in the direction of Manassas Junction, and Jackson's Corps was pressing on to get in Pope's rear, while the cavalry marched between, protecting Jackson's right flank.

The object of the movement was, if possible, to cut off Pope and capture the vast supplies which had been accumulated at Manassas Junction.

During the two or three days before the great battle of Second Bull Run was fought, we were constantly engaged in skirmishing and harassing the enemy.

Colonel Henderson, in the "Life of Jackson," described the cavalry fight which took place on the afternoon of the 30th of August as probably the most brilliant sabre charge in the war.

My company, commanded by Capt. Ridgely Brown,—first company in front, Second Virginia Cavalry, Army of Northern Virginia,—was ordered to reconnoitre and report.

General Lee was already pressing Pope's army, and Stuart's cavalry was stationed on the extreme right, ready to take advantage of any opportunity to charge the retreating enemy. We were not long in sending back word to Colonel Munford that several regiments of Federal cavalry were in our immediate front. Colonel Munford and his regiment came up at a dashing gait, forming front into line, our company on the right.

Colonel Broadhead, commanding the Sixth Michigan Cavalry, moved out to take the same position just in front of us. Here stood the two opposing regiments, within one hundred yards of each other, face to face. The excitement was intense. We were ordered to fight with sabres, and the command, "Draw sabres, forward, trot, gallop, charge!" rang out from both commanders.

Colonel Broadhead was killed and Colonel Munford received a sabre cut over the head. The two regiments locked sabres. Almost immediately support from both sides dashed into the fight. The dust and confusion became so great as to make it almost impossible to distinguish friend from foe.

I had joined the cavalry only a few weeks before, and it was my first cavalry fight. Unfortunately for me, my sabre, a poor specimen of Confederate iron, was soon bent and quite useless. I was attacked by three Yankees. I was fighting for my life, when kindly aid came from one of my comrades by the name of Nelson, who cut down two of my opponents, and at the third I made a

A CONFEDERATE CAVALRY TROOPER,
AS SKETCHED BY A. C. REDWOOD

right cut which missed him, and which nearly unhorsed me. Scarcely recovering my seat, I saw an officer coming straight at me tierce-point.

I had only a moment to gather my thoughts, and in that moment my pistol was leveled at him, to surrender or die. He threw up his hands and surrendered—horse, foot and dragoon. He was an officer of one of the Michigan cavalry regiments. During the remainder of the war I rode in his saddle. His sabre I presented to my cousin, Capt. James Shaw Franklin, of the Second Maryland Infantry.

I may here tell a story of my old friend, Bob Keene. His horse ran away in the charge, and it was not until late that night that he found his way back to camp, without horse, sword or hat, and said that, to escape being captured, he had crawled into a hollow tree, and had remained their until everything was quiet.

Every word of this was true, for Bob Keene was a brave fellow, and it was not fear of the enemy that put him in this plight.

The following day Colonel Munford's regiment moved to Leesburg. As soon as we got there we engaged the enemy in the streets. Meem's Partisan Rangers, numbering six hundred men, were routed and most of them captured. I was fortunate in capturing a live Yankee and a good horse, ridding myself of the old scrub which I had purchased a few months before while at Staunton, Va.

I was now well mounted and well equipped with Yankee sabre, Yankee saddle, Yankee boots and Yankee horse, ready for the Maryland campaign of 1862.

Gen. Fitz Lee, in command of the Confederate cavalry, preceded the army into Maryland. My company was still attached to the Second Virginia. We crossed the river at Edwards's Ferry, marching in the direction of Frederick City, taking up position in a little town called Urbana.

We were to guard General Lee's right flank against any sudden attack of the enemy approaching from the direction of Washington.

Lee was concentrating his army in the vicinity of Frederick City, moving on the road to Boonesboro' and Hagerstown, and crossing South Mountain at Crampton's Gap. Lee had sent Jackson by Turner's Gap to capture Harper's Ferry, which was accomplished in fine style.

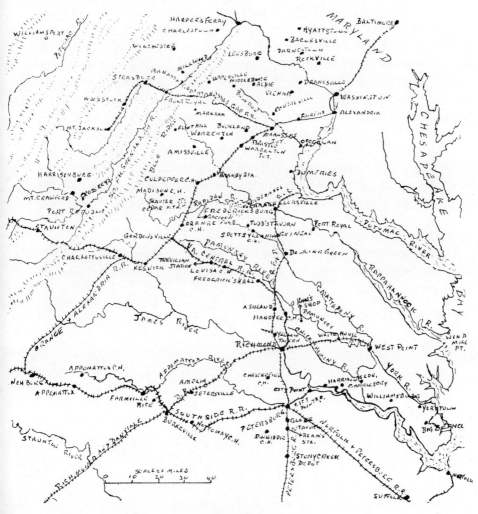

WAR ZONE

Courtesy Official Military Atlas of the Civil War

Our company was still attached to Munford's regiment, bringing up the rear of Lee's army. We all enjoyed the kindly reception received from the citizens of Frederick. They were hospitable and liberal in their donations of good things.

Up to this time we had not been pressed by the enemy. In passing through Crampton's Gap, however, the Yankee cavalry overtook our regiment. They greatly outnumbered us; in fact, they were supported by Franklin's Division of Infantry, and soon drove us from our position. We suffered severely in this fight. Lee's army was forming on the west bank of Antietam Creek, awaiting the return of Jackson. McClellan moved cautiously when he should have moved with great rapidity. Finally there ensued one of the most sanguinary and bloody battles of the war,—the battle of Antietam.

Our command in this fight occupied a position to the extreme right of the army, and while we witnessed a stubbornly contested struggle for two days, we were not actively engaged ourselves. We could, however, see the desperate fighting going on on both sides, without being exposed to it.

Our army retired across the Potomac without being further molested by the enemy. On this march our company brought up the rear.

CHAPTER VII

RAIDS ON THE ENEMY ——————————————

On returning to Virginia we were ordered to take position near Snicker's Ferry, on the Shenandoah River. We picketed for some weeks on the river.

Major Charles Lewis lived near by, and, with his charming wife, entertained us most hospitably for the few weeks we were in the vicinity of the old Shenandoah Springs, quite a noted place in days gone by.

Here we were enabled to give our horses a much needed rest, and we amused ourselves, when not on picket duty, by shooting partridges and different kinds of game.

We were ordered from this point to Leesburg, and arrived there one Sunday evening at dark. The girls were delighted to see this splendid regiment of Virginians and Marylanders, and ran out of their houses to kiss our horses, but I will not say how many of the men kissed the girls.

Capt. Frank A. Bond, in a recent letter to me, recalls the fact that my mess had a lot of pies made of preserves. We had ordered more pies than we could eat, and as we had to break camp the following morning, we invited the officers to participate in our frugal repast. It was just at this time that I met with a very serious loss. My horse, which I valued very highly, developed a fistula, and I had to leave him to his fate. No one except a cavalryman knows how deeply one becomes attached to his animal, which has carried him safely through so many perilous and dangerous encounters in war.

I abandoned him in a good field of grass, and I hope he finally got well, to render to some one else the same good service that he had done to me.

We were now getting into the autumn months, beautiful October, and our company was encamped at Winchester, under command of Gen. George H. Steuart, who was subsequently relieved by Gen. William E. Jones.

For the past three months we had been the first company in front of the Second Virginia Cavalry, and during this time we had achieved a reputation quite enviable in the army. Colonel Munford had frequently applauded our company for its conduct in battle, and we were loath to part from such good friends.

There were, however, several Maryland companies organizing for the purpose of forming the First Maryland Battalion of Cavalry, and three of them came together at Winchester for this purpose, and elected our Captain, Ridgely Brown, major of the battalion.

The weather continued beautiful, and we remained a while longer in the neighborhood of Winchester, picketing on the Romney road, at the gap in the mountains several miles away. Here we could get fine pheasant shooting, and in this way amused ourselves before going into winter quarters. After the first of December we moved up the Valley near Edenburg.

Here another company joined the battalion, and we went into permanent winter quarters. We had daily drills, and improvised a race-track. We had many exciting races, at other times played cards, etc.

On one occasion two of my comrades, Gustav Lurman and Charlie Inloes, introduced a "vingt-et-un bank." The men were flush, having just been paid off. I had never seen the game played, but after watching it for a short time, I concluded to take a hand. I was most successful in all my ventures, winning upwards of $1,200 in Confederate money, which broke the bank for the time being. The next morning, however, additional capital was secured, and the game started afresh, although I was not permitted to play, as they were afraid of my good luck.

On January 2d, 1863, a bitter cold day, the whole brigade started on an expedition to Moorefield, marching all day and all night, crossing the mountians. Many men were frostbitten. Both of my heels were badly nipped, but I soon recovered. We had expected to encounter the enemy near Moorefield. The suffering of the men was intense, and General Jones became very unpopular for this movement.

On February 23d, our company, under command of Captain Bond, was informed by one of Jones' scouts that a company of Yankee cavalry, picketing near Winchester, could be easily captured.

An expedition was made up, and we started on a cold, chilly afternoon, reckoning to reach the outlying pickets about midnight. Led by a faithful guide, we arrived at the expected time, and succeeded in working our way to the rear of the command, resulting in the capture of the entire Yankee company.

Accomplishing this, we started at a trot to get away with our prisoners. We felt sure the enemy would pursue, and, as expected, they were soon on our track. We quickened our pace from trot to gallop. Captain Bond, with the usual foresight of a good officer, dispatched two of his men to inform General Jones that one or two regiments were closing in on us, and to be ready to meet them when we came up.

We were in no condition to fight after a gallop of nearly eighty-seven miles. General Jones had promptly ordered the Seventh Cavalry to mount, and before we reached New Market they were moving down the turnpike, nicely closed up and ready for the charge. This was fun for the Virginians.

Those who had been pursuing us through the night, without due regard to the risk of being attacked, had strung themselves out for miles along the pike, and the Virginians, coming out fresh and well closed up, soon made havoc among them, capturing, wounding, and killing three hundred men.

It was a most successful raid on our part, and Captain Bond was complimented for the manner in which he had handled the expedition.

It was while I was in winter quarters that I had the pleasure of making the acquaintance of Capt. George Blackford, one of Lee's most noted scouts, who was temporarily assigned to duty in the Valley of Virginia.

Captain Blackford invited me to accompany him on a little expedition down the Valley, to capture a wagon-train of the enemy, which was in the habit of passing daily between Winchester and Berryville. There were six of us in all, and we had been informed that five four-horse teams, with a quartermaster, drivers and an escort of three cavalrymen, generally composed the party, and would pass a given point about 2 o'clock in the afternoon.

On each side of the turnpike between Winchester and Berryville, where it crosses the Opequon, the banks were very high. It was at this point that we concluded to make the attack. Our horses were securely tied in the woods, thirty or forty yards in our rear, and we crawled up to the crest of the hill, and, peeping over the banks, waited for the approach of the wagon-train.

We were not long in suspense. Captain Blackford had ordered three of us to fall upon the enemy in front, and three in rear, with cocked revolvers, and to shoot immediately if we met with any resistance.

We captured the whole train. Each Yankee driver was ordered to lead out his team and three cavalrymen to dismount. A side road was within fifty yards of us, where we had tied our horses, and the whole party was away in a jiffy.

The wagons, with the supplies, were abandoned. We could not attempt to carry them off over the rough roads. Our prize consisted in all of twenty-three horses and seven prisoners. We pressed on to Millwood and Front Royal that night, passing north under cover of the Massanutton Mountain. We reached New Market the following morning with our prisoners and horses.

A few days later Captain Blackford came into camp and handed me six hundred dollars in gold as my share of the proceeds of the sale of the horses. This was a privilege accorded to scouts and not to regular army officers and privates. Money of this kind I always sent to my banker in Richmond, to be applied equally for credit of my brother and myself, the former being in the infantry. This gave us plenty of money for some months to come, and enabled us to keep up a respectable outfit.

Shortly after this time, during the month of April, I was suddenly taken sick with a bilious attack, and could not go with my company on the West Virginia expedition to Greenland's Gap.

I spent most of the time in bed at Mrs. Thomas Jordan's house, in Luray, Va., and she was very kind and good to me. I soon recovered, however, and rejoined my company on its return to the Valley, about the first of June, 1863.

We were detached at this point from the Maryland Battalion, and ordered to report to General Ewell as his body-guard. The old brigade, under command of General Jones, had been ordered east of the Blue Ridge to join General Stuart's command in the vicinity of Culpeper C. H.

Gen. Robert E. Lee was evidently concentrating his whole army in this vicinity, some twenty miles south of Winchester, preparatory to another invasion of Maryland and Pennsylvania.

Milroy was at Winchester and Berryville, and Ewell was moving on Winchester with his corps. It took position for battle on the morning of June 14th, Early leading the attack. Johnson's Division had been moved north of Winchester that night to anticipate, if possible, any attempt of Milroy to escape towards Martinsburg, but Johnson could not reach his position in time to intercept Milroy. He got away with a small body of troops on the road to Harper's Ferry.

The next morning Winchester surrendered, leaving in our hands several thousand prisoners, and a large quantity of stores, cannon, wagons and horses. It was a complete destruction of Milroy's army.

To be assigned to duty at the headquarters of a general commanding a corps was quite an elevation for us. We anticipated pleasant military experiences, which were more than realized before we got through the Gettysburg campaign.

At Hagerstown, where a number of our men resided prior to the war, they met old friends and relatives, and were most royally treated. At Chambersburg and Carlisle, although in the enemy's country, we received many smiles from the girls peeping through the windows. No damage of any kind was done to property, and the citizens generally looked upon us as a rather civilized and well-behaved crowd.

Captain Bond was authorized by General Ewell to make occasional scouts in the vicinity, to replenish our larder or pick up something good for the boys. We invited ourselves one day to dine at a good-looking house, with big barns and well-stored granaries. We ventured to order a dinner for ten. At first the old lady was rather reluctant to obey our Captain's command. She did not relish working for a lot of rebels, but seeing that we meant business and intended to have the dinner, she finally got to work and really set up for us a most satisfying repast within a short time.

We saw some very pretty girls in the kitchen, doubtless the daughters of the old lady, squinting at us from time to time, but whenever perceived that we could see them, they "skedaddled" out of sight.

We all sat down to dinner, and expressed ourselves as great-ly pleased with the hospitality of the landlady; we told her we should be very glad to see the young ladies, that we were not bar-barians, and that they would be surprised to see how nicely we could act towards them, if they would come up and wait on us. The old lady opened the door and cried out, "Come up, girls; these rebel boys are not as bad as you think," and in a few minutes the girls were all up and having a jolly time with us. I think they forgot in a short time that we were enemies of their country and destroyers of their homes. Several flirtations occurred, and all sorts of promises to return after the war were made. These girls were really loath to bid us adieu, and waved their handkerchiefs at us as long as we were in sight, and they frequently said, "How could you be so nice and be a rebel?"

Two days later we were drawn up in line of battle in front of Gettysburg. This was the first day's fight. The battle broke over that beautiful valley about three o'clock in the afternoon. Ewell had thrown his men against the Eleventh Army Corps, and by four o'clock the whole Confederate line was driving the enemy before it. General Reynolds was killed in this fight. Captain Bond, leading his company, was among the first to charge into Gettysburg.

General Ewell the next morning appointed Captain Bond Pro-vost Marshal of the town. We all did active service throughout the entire three days' fight, and on the night of July 4th, the night of the withdrawal of Lee's army from Gettysburg, we were deployed in front of Ewell's line as pickets, to remain in our saddles until relieved. Those of us who were there will never forget that night. The dead had been exposed to the broiling sun for more than twenty-four hours, and had already turned black.

To add to the horror of the scene and the cries and groans of dying men, in the midst of whom we stood, a terrible thunder and lightning storm broke over the battle-field. The rain fell in torrents, and as each of us stood at his post, with pistol in hand, the lightning flashed in our faces casting shadows on the dead strewn around us. Here we remained until day dawned. Who can forget that night! Our sergeant passed down the line, forming us into columns of fours, preparatory to marching off the battle-field.

We continued as General Ewell's body-guard until we ap-proached Hagerstown, where we rejoined our battalion. In the streets of Hagerstown we encountered a Federal regiment of cavalry, and fought with them in hand-to-hand combat. I shall never forget the magnificent conduct of Sergeant Hammond Dorsey, of our company. With his strong arm he wielded his sabre like Hercules, cutting down many of the enemy from their horses.

We drove them back on the road to Boonesboro', and in another encounter, later in the same evening, our gallant Captain was cut down from his horse with a serious wound in his left leg, compelling his absence from us for several months, while suffering severely from his wound.

We were all "bottled up" with General Lee's army for some days at Williamsport, owing to the high water of the Potomac. General Lee fortified his position, and would have given battle to General Meade if he had attempted to press us beyond this point.

I have a very indistinct recollection of what occurred across the river; in fact, there was no fighting of any consequence. General Lee gradually retired towards Winchester and then to Culpeper, our command extending as far as Fredericksburg on our extreme right.

I was called to Gen. Fitz Lee's headquarters as a courier in the fall of 1863. We were then stationed near Fredericksburg, Colonel Bradley T. Johnson in command of our battalion. I had always wished to serve under Lee, although at that time I knew him only by reputation. The whole cavalry corps looked upon him as an eminently able young officer, and one who would rise rapidly in the estimation of the army.

I felt that I might have a chance here. I certainly did my part, but promotion was slow to Marylanders without friends or influence.

General Lee's headquarters at that time were about three miles distant from Fredericksburg, at Guest's house, on the old plank road.

I suppose I was indebted for this slight elevation to Capt. Henry Lee, brother of Gen. Fitz Lee, a classmate of mine at the University of Virginia prior to the war. From the beginning I formed a most agreeable association with Gen. Lee, his staff, couriers and members of the Signal Corps, which has lasted these many years, and it is a great pleasure to me, whenever the opportunity offers, of coming together with these old comrades. General Lee, recognizing my desire not only to serve my country, but to make for

Capt. William E. Rasin,
Co. E, 1st Battalion, Maryland Cavalry, C.S.A.
A fellow member of John Gill's battalion.
Courtesy Confederate Museum

GEN. FITZHUGH LEE, NEPHEW OF ROBERT E. LEE.
Courtesy Library of Congress

myself a place and position at his headquarters, promoted me, after the Culpeper fight, to the rank of sergeant of the Signal Corps. I participated in all the important engagements which took place during the autumn of 1863, and shortly after the fight at Mine Run, our division went into winter quarters at Charlottesville.

I recall with much pride the magnificent conduct of our cavalry division, under command of Gen. Fitz Lee, in the attack on Kilpatrick's Division at Culpeper and Brandy Station; and then again at Buckland, on the Warrenton Road. I could not resist the opportunity of going in with our men in a great charge, which took place in the railroad cut near Brandy Station, where we flanked the enemy. I brought out a Yankee sergeant, who turned over to me a very handsome Colt's revolver, which I presented to General Lee.

CHAPTER VIII

SPOTSYLVANIA C. H., TREVILIAN STATION TO CITY POINT ————

Our command, after wintering at Charlottesville, where Gen. Fitz Lee devoted a great deal of time to the reorganization of the cavalry division, to make it more effective in the spring campaign of '64, moved to the vicinity of Fredericksburg.

It was about this time that General Grant, who had assumed command of the Federal forces, and whose intention was to attack General Lee, began his great move to the Wilderness, Chancellorsville and North Anna, culminating in his overwhelming check at Cold Harbor.

The cavalry at this time was most actively engaged guarding both flanks of Lee's army. Our division was thrown in front at Spottsylvania Court House until Longstreet's Corps could come up. This was one of the severest fights in which we ever engaged.

We were driven back to the temporary barricade put up by our infantry. It was at this point that Colonel Collins, of the Fifteenth Virginia Cavalry, was killed, and Major Mason and I were ordered by General Lee to bring out his body. There was great confusion at the moment, and we were being pressed to the rear by the advancing line of Federal infantry. I dismounted, and, with the assistance of Mason, tried to lift Collins to my saddle, but failed in doing so, and, under heavy fire, we were compelled to leave him between the battle-lines. After remounting, I had to jump a high barricade, and in the act my horse, a noted piebald stallion, was killed.

General Lee was moving his army by the right flank, chastising Grant severely whenever he attempted to turn it.

We were now constantly engaging the enemy, and were in the saddle day and night. In a little skirmish near Taylorsville, Hanover County, we encountered the Fifth United States Regulars, attacked and routed them. In this fight our handsome young courier, Tom Burke, was shot through the leg, a tender lad of scarcely twenty years, as pretty as a picture, with rosy cheeks. We heard the bullet strike him. It was no joke, but he bore it like a man and behaved like a veteran.

The next day the memorable cavalry fight at Yellow Tavern took place. Sheridan came with overwhelming numbers. We lost the gallant Jeb Stuart, the commander-in-chief of our cavalry, but Sheridan was foiled in his attempt to capture Richmond.

It was a desperate fight along the entire line. General Stuart was wounded and was brought off the field by some of the gallant members of Company K, First Virginia Cavalry. I am proud to say that this company was commanded by Capt. Gus Dorsey, of Howard County, Maryland, and was composed principally of Marylanders.

Major Ferguson, our chief of staff, had his horse shot under him in the fight, and in the confusion the members of our headquarters staff were widely scattered.

I was standing on the Richmond road, our cavalry having just been driven back to the right, when Stuart was wounded. That night I saw him placed in an ambulance. He insisted upon being taken to his wife. I have always felt that Stuart might have lived if he had been kept quiet that night. In a few days the report came of his death. This was a great loss to the country, an irreparable loss to the cavalry. Jackson had died just a year before. Thus two of our greatest commanders had "passed over the river" in so short a time.

On May 23d we were at Atlee's Station. In the afternoon we moved to Kenyon's farm, on the Lower James, opposite Brandon, for the purpose of breaking up an encampment of negro troops, who had fortified quite extensively at a point known as Harrison's Landing. We reached the place about one o'clock. I had command of headquarter couriers in driving in the pickets and led the charge.

There were about ten of us against a company of negroes on picket. Willie McFarland, of Richmond, Va., a very warm, personal friend of mine, and a member of my signal corps, killed a negro in this charge. The rest surrendered without further resistance.

I carried a message from General Lee, under flag of truce, to the commander of the fort, to surrender. This was refused by Brigadier-General Wild, in command, and I was told to say to General Lee, "Take the fort if you can." This garrison consisted of three regiments of colored troops, and a number of transports and gunboats were in the river in reserve.

On my return I was asked if the fort could be taken, and I replied that it could not. I had been so close to it, surrounded as it was by a moat, that my mind was quickly made up that any attempt, even to attack, would prove disastrous. However, the order was given to dismount, and two lines formed. As we approached the fort the negroes, with uncovered heads, rose above the intrenchments and leveled their guns upon us. I could see the glint of the sun reflected on their teeth and their polished rifle-barrels. Then came a cloud of smoke, bullets whizzed through our ranks, and the men in our lines tumbled over each other, some forward, some backward. Our fire was ineffective, and they poured volley after volley into our waning ranks. Finally our lines broke and retreated, and we left many dead and wounded on the field. In addition to the effective firing from the fort, several gunboats opened on us, and stampeded our horses. We encamped that night on the Charles City road, near White's Tavern, where we received rations and corn from Richmond.

On May 28th we had a severe fight at Hawes' Shop, where we encountered the enemy in force, and engaged them sharply. We found Yankee cavalry, supported by Yankee infantry, in our front.

The Charleston Dragoons, a splendid body of young men, fresh from their homes, well mounted, became engaged with the enemy. We soon discovered that they were confronted by a line of solid infantry. General Lee sent me to withdraw them. Several of the staff said "Good-bye," as, in obedience to orders, I rode at full speed to the rescue.

Bullets were flying thick and fast, and were thinning out the ranks of this battalion; yet they continued fighting desperately against great odds.

I had not time to address the Colonel. I gave the order, as I broke into their ranks, "Right about face, double quick, march," and succeeded in extricating them from a very dangerous position. General Lee complimented me for the prompt manner in which I had acted, and I was also congratulated on all sides on having come out myself unscathed. I think Colonel Rutledge or Colonel Donovan commanded this battalion.

There was no fighting the following day, the division remaining several days in the vicinity of Atlee's Station. During all this time Gen. Robert E. Lee was stubbornly and successfully resisting the efforts of Grant to turn his right flank.

On June first the cavalry moved across the Chickahominy towards Seven Pines, in the vicinity of Bottom's Bridge. That afternoon both infantry and cavalry became engaged, General Ewell attacking and driving the enemy from his front.

Breckenridge's Division came up and we were relieved. On June 3d there was heavy fighting along the entire line. Grant was handsomely repulsed, and many prisoners were taken. At this time the cavalry had most important service to render, to keep General Lee advised as to whether or not Grant intended crossing the James River, and if so, at what point.

The movement of the cavalry was so rapid in those days that it was a rare thing to find division headquarters wagons up at night. We generally made headquarters at some farmer's house, and these people, although greatly impoverished by the war, always gave us the best they had.

The following day the division was ordered to Ashland, within sixteen miles of Richmond, and here we were joined by Butler's Brigade. We learned that a large force of cavalry, under Sheridan, had encamped the night before at Atlett's, in Caroline County.

The scouts reported that Sheridan's column was marching to join Hunter in the Valley. We left Ashland on the afternoon of the 9th, and encamped that night near Trinity Church, made an early start the next morning for Frederickshall, halted there three hours, resumed the march, and encamped at night near Louisa C. H. Sheridan's cavalry encamped within three miles of us.

June 11th we were in the saddle at 3 A.M., encountered the enemy before daylight, and fighting continued throughout the day. I was in the charge that broke Custer's line and captured his headquarters wagons and Colonel Pennington's Horse Artillery.

A few years ago, while visiting Fortress Monroe, I had the pleasure of meeting General Pennington, and of informing him

GENERAL WADE HAMPTON LEADS THE "CADET CHARGE" AT THE LOUISA COUNTY COURT HOUSE WHICH WAS THE PRELUDE TO THE BATTLE OF TREVILIAN STATION, 11-12 JUNE 1864. THIS WAS THE GREATEST AND BLOODIEST ALL CAVALRY BATTLE OF THE WAR.
Courtesy of the Archives — Museum, The Citadel, Charleston, S.C.

Cadets from The Citadel College were a unit of the 6th South Carolina Cavalry and were a part of this fight to repel Union Cavalry that was attacking Hart's Artillery Battery. The troops repelled the advance and saved the artillery and Louisa Court House from capture.

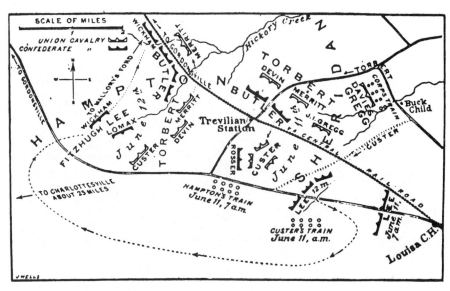

MAP OF THE BATTLE OF TREVILIAN STATION
Courtesy Battles and Leaders of the Civil War

After a two day struggle, Confederate Major General Wade Hampton's outnumbered troopers, numbering about 5,000, defeated Major General Philip Sheridan's superior equipped forces of about 8,000 men in the greatest and bloodiest all cavalry battle of the war. Sheridan's casualties totaled 1,007 while Hampton's are estimated to be 1,071.

Hampton followed the retreating invaders day after day and in the hundred miles of road between Trevilians and the White House on the Pamunkey River two thousand horses were found shot through the head—twenty per mile.

LT. ALEXANDER C. M. PENNINGTON,
2ND U.S. ARTILLERY, U.S.A.
Courtesy Library of Congress

*John Gill was in the charge that broke General George Custer's advance
and captured his Headquarters wagons along with Lieutenant A. C. M. Pennington's Horse Artillery. He took as a trophy a handsome buffalo robe
from Pennington's wagon.*

ARTIFACTS FOUND AT THE TREVILIAN STATION BATTLEFIELD
BY ELTON STRONG OF MINERAL, VA.
Courtesy Elton Strong

that on that occasion my trophy in the battle was a handsome buffalo robe. I had taken this robe from Pennington's wagon, and I laughingly remarked that, if he still wanted it, there was a lady in Richmond by the name of Miss Mason who would doubtless return it to him.

I also had the pleasure of talking to Captain Green, Custer's adjutant-general, who was captured in this fight, and to whom I extended some slight service on the battle-field.

Some years afterwards I had the pleasure of meeting him in Baltimore. He recalled my kindness to him, remembered my name, and came into my office to meet and thank me again.

Trevilians was a desperate encounter, with varying success to both sides, but finally terminated in Sheridan's retreat.

Hampton followed him in hot pursuit. Our division, however, moved into Trevilians Station the next morning to find a large number of prisoners and wounded men left on the field. Orders were given to establish a hospital and to see that the men received proper attention. Their friends had left them to our care.

That night, after a march of nearly twenty miles, we encamped again in the vicinity of Frederickshall. In speaking of the battle of Trevilians, I am reminded of many sad memories. Up to this time in almost every engagement in which we fought, we had been successful. We had whipped and routed the enemy upon many a field. Now the tide was turning. No longer had we the men, horses or provender with which to make this branch of the service effective. The history of the cavalry of the Army of Northern Virginia, under Stuart, Hampton and Lee, will, however, stand forever distinguished for its many achievements.

General Sheridan, with inexhaustible resources, was daily adding to his magnificently equipped corps. From this time on we had no means of maintaining our former efficiency. Sheridan was indefatigable, never idle. Within two days we learned he was again on the move. It was almost impossible to keep up with him, and we were on the lookout day and night. The whole line of march was perfumed with dead horses.

It was just at this time that we were experiencing the most trying conditions of the war. On June 23d we were ordered into saddle at 1 A.M. We moved out across White Oak Swamp, and from thence to Charles City C. H.

A portion of our division that afternoon engaged Gregg's Division. Notwithstanding the excessive fatigue of the men, Gregg was driven back in confusion and pursued for five miles until dark.

Major Breathed, a distinguished Marylander, of whom I shall have more to say later on, killed Colonel Covode, of the Fourth Pennsylvania Cavalry.

In the vicinity of the James River, a malarial country, we suffered from intensely hot weather, and for the want of food and rest, watching Grant's movements, to ascertain at what point he would cross the river or whether he would retreat to Yorktown.

I cannot recall what occurred daily during this hot weather, but we were constantly on the march. About July 1st we crossed the James River, and marched to Petersburg, and from there to Reams' Station, on the Weldon Railroad.

I now reach a very important cavalry fight. General Wilson, commanding a division of Federal cavalry, was raiding in our rear. We were ordered in pursuit, and were soon in close touch with him. We were brought into action early in the morning, just after Mahone had captured most of his artillery.

We became hotly engaged, forcing the enemy before us, and destroyed most of his wagons, caissons and ammunition. We soon discovered that it was a raid of depredation and cruelty. No respect was paid to private property or to the homes of the defenceless. It developed that more than three thousand negroes were following in the wake of the cavalry and that the majority of the soldiers were loaded with stolen household articles of some kind or other, particularly bed-clothing and wearing apparel. Negro women were seen throwing their little babies ruthlessly aside. Our men became greatly enraged, and it was difficult to restrain them. It was a question of quarter or no quarter, and it was mostly no quarter. I had just returned from the right of our line, where I had witnessed dozens of Yankees shot down in the act of plundering private houses and insulting helpless women, when I hastened to the front with orders from General Lee to keep him advised of what was going on.

I was with Major Breathed at the head of the charging column when he fell wounded. General Lee and Major Ferguson rode up, and everything was done for Breathed that could be done. Fortunately he was not dangerously wounded, although at the time

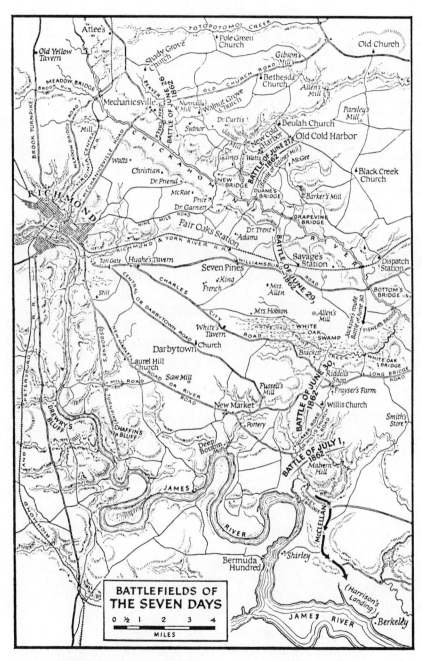

BATTLEFIELDS OF THE SEVEN DAYS

0 ½ 1   2   3   4

MILES

Courtesy Clifford Dowdey, Richmond, Va.

the wound was supposed to be fatal. He rejoined his command within a few weeks. We continued in pursuit of the enemy all day until late at night, camping in the vicinity of Jarratt's Landing. It was a day of horrors. We witnessed the cruelty of warfare in almost every phase. The poor negro women who had left their homes in the hope of obtaining their freedom remained screaming along the roads and in the forests through the night.

As we pressed the enemy, we found the roads strewn with every description of cavalry equipment, wearing apparel, dead men and dead horses, and every variety of stolen property from a negro down to a brooch.

That night, when I was about ready to rest my tired head, Gen. Fitz Lee said: "Gill, I want you to take despatches to Gen. Robert E. Lee, headquarters Appomattox, opposite Petersburg."

I can never forget that night. The stars were shining brightly, but I was in a strange land, and I might say far from home, fully twenty-five to thirty miles from General Lee's headquarters. I told General Lee that it was almost impossible for me to find my way to Petersburg. General Lee said: "You have the best bump of locality of anyone at headquarters. There is the North star; follow it until you reach the Dinwiddie C. H. plank road. Turn sharp to the right, and you will be on the road to Petersburg."

Little did I think what I would have to endure that night. After a ride of a few miles from camp I found the road and the woods resounding with the screams of negro women and the groans of dying men. This made night hideous. I pressed on, however, with my revolver cocked, not knowing at what moment I should be shot down. All kinds of appeals were made to me, but I never stopped. About two o'clock in the morning I crossed the Dinwiddie plank road.

If anything, that night was more trying than the night we stood picket in front of Gettysburg.

I reached General Lee's headquarters about 6:30 in the morning, and delivered my despatches. No one asked me to breakfast. I returned to Reams' Station, about twelve miles away, hungry, tired, and with nothing to eat, reaching camp about noon. Gen. Fitz Lee and his division came up the following day.

A few days later I met Stringfellow, General Lee's popular scout, and in response to an invitation from him, with six or seven other men, I accompanied him on one of his expeditions within the enemy's lines. The first night was spent in the dismal swamp near City Point. We were almost devoured by mosquitoes. Our faces the next morning were badly disfigured. I have always been under the impression that we were lost that night. It was cloudy, and we could not take our bearings, and I think that we sought the swamp for safety. We started early the next morning, and just as we struck the road leading to City Point, we came face to face with a squad of eight or nine Yankee cavalrymen. We charged them at once and routed them, capturing three prisoners. My horse was shot through the neck in the melee but I managed to get back to camp with him. Thus ended this little exploit.

CHAPTER IX

FIGHTING IN THE VALLEY ————————————

On July 29th we broke camp and marched towards Richmond. The next morning we were ordered back, owing doubtless to the explosion of the crater on our lines. We returned to our old encampment near Reams' Station. Here we learned that Hampton was fighting south of us on our right.

Again, on August 5th, we were ordered to Richmond, and continued the march to Ashland. From Ashland we marched across the South Anna River, and encamped late that evening. Here we found recent newspapers from the North, acknowledging the failure of Grant's campaign against Richmond and Petersburg.

The head of our column was turned towards Culpeper; evidently we were again on the march to the Valley. From Culpeper we marched to Flint Hill and across the Blue Ridge at Chester Gap, halting at Front Royal.

Our division met the enemy in the vicinity of Front Royal, but being at headquarters, I did not participate in any fighting.

News came to us on the 20th of August of the death of General Chambliss, who had fallen near Richmond. He was a popular officer, and dearly beloved by everyone.

In the Valley General Early was in command of the army, and we remained inactive almost up to the date of the battle of Winchester. We knew that Sheridan was preparing to move on Winchester. That memorable battle took place on the 19th of September, in which we were badly whipped.

Some one erred in this fight. It seem ridiculous to engage Sheridan with an army of 39,000 opposed to our 12,000 men. Perhaps if Early had kept his three divisions in close touch the result might have been different. I witnessed the entire Confederate line give way. I had been sent to Stevenson's Depot to withdraw Lomax, and we all came back at a gallop with the Yankee cavalry close on our heels.

General Fitz Lee displayed conspicuous gallantry in his efforts to rally the cavalry, and was shot, himself, after having two horses go down under him in quick succession. He was badly wounded. It was almost a miracle that he escaped capture. Had it not been for several members of his staff, who stood by him and got him off the field, he would have been in the hands of the enemy.

Captain Cavendish and I, together with a number of headquarters men, charged at the head of the 6th Virginia Regiment, hoping to check the enemy for the moment to enable the infantry to reform its lines under the gallant Gordon of Georgia.

Sheridan virtually drove us through Winchester, and it would be very difficult for many of us to recall where we slept that night, but we managed to get together the next morning, when, under orders from Major J. D. Ferguson, Chief of our staff, we reported to General Wickham, then temporarily assigned to the command of our division.

We never witnessed a worse condition of affairs or worse demoralization among our troops, resulting from the defeat at Winchester, as well as the defeat which followed two days later at Fisher's Hill. Here was a strong position and should have been held, but for some lack of generalship, or for some other reason, Sheridan broke in our left, precipitating another disastrous rout.

After this experience I always felt like giving a groan when I had to fight under Early. If Gordon had commanded the army, with Fitz Lee commanding the cavalry, the result might have been very different.

The retreat continued up the Valley in the direction of Staunton. We were skirmishing daily. Although only a sergeant in charge of the Signal Corps and our couriers, I managed to make a good impression on General Wickham.

On the morning of the 27th or 28th of September, we were sharply engaged with the enemy near a little town by the name of Vienna, not far from Port Republic. We had just come out of the Luray Valley. The officer commanding the skrimishers was shot down. General Wickham turned quickly to me, and said: "Go, and take command of that line." This was a recognition which I had long sought. In a jiffy I was at my post.

With the exception of myself, the cavalrymen were dismounted. We held the enemy in check, although greatly outnumbered. I had only been there a few minutes when I heard a bullet strike my favorite horse, Red Eye. I scanned his right side, but could not see where the bullet had penetrated. It was all over, however, in a few minutes, when the gallant charger fell to his knees and rolled over on his left side, and I stepped to the ground.

I remained in command until the afternoon. The infantry retired towards Brown's Gap, while the cavalry moved towards Waynesboro' I was fortunate enough, although under fire, to remove my saddle and bridle and get them to the rear. It was the same old saddle captured in the cavalry charge at Second Bull Run, which I valued very highly.

I got back to headquarters late that night. We encamped near Waynesboro'. Next morning I asked General Wickham for three days' leave of absence to go to Richmond, to get sufficient money to remount myself, which leave was granted.

I arrived in Richmond October 1st, 1864. At that time Confederate money was almost valueless. I succeeded, however, in negotiating a draft for one hundred dollars in greenbacks, payable in Baltimore, for which I received thirty-five hundred dollars in Confederate currency.

I should mention that I had drawn this draft on my mother, who rebuked me in several of her recent "underground" letters for not drawing more frequently. It was my rule, however, never to ask for money from my dear mother unless I was sick, or for some such purpose as just stated.

I had seen the abuse of this privilege early in the war on the part of many gallant Marylanders, who had come South with the best intentions, but who were ruined by dissipation and riotous living at the Confederate capital.

My finances being satisfactorily arranged, I strolled up the main street in Richmond to the Spottswood Hotel. Here I met some old comrades, among whom was George Lemmon. I greeted him most cordially, but was shocked to note the expression of his face. Something surely had happened. Lemmon told me of my brother's death. He had fallen the day before in a desperate encounter with the enemy in front of Reams' Station.

That gallant and heroic band of young Marylanders for the second time, as at Culp's Hill, had been slaughtered by the enemy. How terrible the blow to me! The dear boy, two years my junior, a lad not yet 20 years of age, the idol of his family, beloved by his comrades and friends, as brave a soldier as ever crossed the Potomac, to die in this way. His body was never recovered. I secured a flag of truce from the Secretary of War, but like all brave soldiers who die on the ramparts of the enemy's works, he is buried in common with the brave who fell on both sides.

Read what a comrade writes about him:

"One of the gallant dead.
Killed in battle by a bullet shot from the hand of the enemy, before Petersburg, Va., September 30th, 1864.
Somerville Pinkney Gill.

"He was one of the best soldiers of the Army of Northern Virginia and that ever crossed the Potomac in defence of his oppressed State as well as the noble Confederacy.

"He died bravely, he was wounded slightly in the shoulder, and was told by his Lieutenant to leave the field. He replied, 'I am only slightly wounded,' and shortly after a bullet pierced his noble forehead and he fell dead.

"He would have been taken off by us, but there were so many wounded to look after that we had to leave him in the hands of the enemy. Such is war, and the good and brave boy has gone from us forever."

"No name, no record! Ask the world,
The world has read his story.
If all his annals can unfold
A prouder tale of glory.
If ever merely human life
Hath taught diviner moral,
If ever round a worthier brow
Was twined a purer laurel."

Being unsuccessful in my effort to recover my brother's body, I returned to our lines to visit the remaining members of his old company. How few of that gallant band were left! We stood and wept upon each other's shoulders before a word was spoken.

I got back to Richmond the same night. I sought no one. In my room at the Spottswood, buried in inconsolable grief, I sat down to break the news to my dear mother. I struggled for hours over my letter, that I might break the news as gently as possible.

I wished I could say, but I could not say, what some have said: "Happily, however, all this is passed, to be seen no more. The fires in that chasm were quenched in Brother's blood."

I arrived in Charlottesville on the morning of October 3d. Here I secured a remount at the cost of $3,000, but he was not equal to old Red Eye or my piebald stallion, shot under me in the battle of Spottsylvania.

Leaving Charlottesville immediately, I pressed on to Harrisonburg to rejoin the cavalry. I caught up with them on the 4th, in the neighborhood of Furrow's Furnace, west of Harrisonburg, and on the road to Warm Springs. Here I found headquarters affairs greatly mixed.

General Wickham had asked for and had been granted a 30 days' leave of absence, and we were ordered to report to General Rosser, now in command of the Division. Rosser learning that the Yankee cavalry was retiring from Harrisonburg, concentrated all his forces and started in pursuit. Rosser made it lively for the cavalry. We had daily encounters with the enemy.

Major Breathed, of the artillery, led in several charges, and returned with his sword red with blood to its hilt. We pressed the enemy down the Valley as far as Fisher's Hill, when the Yankees the following day turned tables on us, driving us pell mell to the rear, flanking us right and left.

Captain Walke, Ordinance Officer of General Lee's staff, was killed in a gallant attempt to rally the men.

CHAPTER X

SKIRMISHES IN MOSBY'S CONFEDERACY————

It was about this time, during the month of October, 1864, that I was taken sick with my third attack of fever, and ordered to the hospital in Richmond. On the train I met the two Misses Thompson of Staunton, Va., Miss Carter, afterwards Mrs. John Lee Carroll, of Maryland, and her sister, who were exceedingly kind to me, and suggested that instead of going to the hospital, I should try to secure a room at the Arlington Hotel.

This was a valuable suggestion, for here I found my old friend, Mrs. Robert Hough, of Baltimore, Mrs. Gen. Joseph E. Johnston, and several other ladies, who cared for me most tenderly during two weeks of catarrhal fever.

When I got out again I remember a charming visit to Petersburg, visiting Col. George Bolling's family during my convalescence. I felt sufficiently restored in health to rejoin the command, which had gone into winter quarters at Waynesboro'.

In many respects it was an extremely sad and gloomy winter, because the inevitable was upon us. We knew that the spring campaign would end the war with the downfall of the Confederacy.

In the winter of 1864-65 Gen. Fitz Lee intrusted me with the command of a scouting party with orders to reconnoitre the Valley of Virginia, then partly in the hands of the Federal forces under Sheridan.

Sheridan and his army had their winter quarters near Winchester, and it behooved us to exercise the greatest vigilance to escape capture.

I recall spending a night some time in March at Major Taylor's plantation on the Shenandoah, where we sought refuge owing to a heavy blizzard or snowstorm. During the night the house was surrounded by Yankees, and if it had not been for a faithful negro man, who assured them that no rebels were there, we should in all probability have been captured.

The old darkey came up into our room, and said the house had been surrounded by Yankees and that we had better get away as soon as we could. One can fancy we were not long in obeying the orders of the old darkey. When we left the house and got into the river road, we heard the clatter of a large cavalry force coming down the road. They evidently knew that we were in the neighborhood and were not satisfied with their previous investigation. Of course, it was not for us to give them fight but to escape as rapidly as possible, and we dashed off for the nearest ford in the river, to cross over to the mountain side.

We were hotly pursued across the river. Pistol shot after pistol shot was fired at us. Fortunately, however, no one was hurt. It was a bitter cold morning, and the dash through the river wet us to the skin. We galloped a mile or more before reaching a habitation of any kind. Here we stopped to dry our clothes, and to get something to eat and a little apple-jack to drive the frost out of our bones.

An old farmer and his wife were the only occupants of the house, and they did everything for our comfort. We were given a large room with a big hickory fire, and in this way dried our clothes. In a few hours we were in condition to continue the march.

We concluded not to risk another trip into the Valley, which was swarming with patroling parties of the enemy. There was nothing left for us to do but to go to Upperville, Fauquier County, and to remain there for a few days before deciding on our future course.

I had now only four men with me. Two of the original party had been sent back with despatches to Gen. Fitzhugh Lee. We were most hospitably received at Upperville by the good people of that little village. We made the acquaintance of a charming family by the name of Stephenson. All the old soldiers who had an eye for a pretty girl will doubtless remember Miss Josephine Stephenson. Then the Harrisons and Bollings were near by, and the Dulanys, on the road to Middleburg, all charming people.

I had the pleasure of being introduced to Captain Glasscock, a captain of Mosby's battalion. I was constantly meeting men of

Mosby's command, all splendid fellows, fine horsemen and gallant soldiers. I was very much pleased with the reception I received from everybody. Captain Glasscock invited McFarland and me to his house. The Captain had inherited a fine estate from his father a few miles from Upperville, and, to add greatly to the agreeable companionship, we met there the Captain who had recently taken to himself a Virginia bride, and we felt that no one could be more fortunate than we were in this opportunity.

Mosby's men were always on the alert, and scarcely a day passed without encountering the enemy at some point. This was only a few weeks before the final surrender at Appomattox.

Glasscock explained to me one morning a little expedition he was getting up to capture a patrol of 22 Yankees, reported as making daily scouts from Georgetown on the road to Vienna in Loudoun County. I gladly availed myself of the opportunity to be with him on this occasion. He took with him about 25 men. Bush Underwood, one of his most trusted lieutenants, was placed in command of the squad which I remained with, while Glasscock, with the rest of the men, took up a position directly on the road about a half-mile beyond where we were hid in the bushes. He would charge them in front, while Underwood would close in rear of the party after they passed the point where we were stationed. It was about midday when the patrol passed up the road. Though they were in full sight of us, we were concealed from them. We waited for the signal from Glasscock to attack, which was one shot from his pistol. The road was enclosed on both sides by a high fence. The minute the signal was given we dashed into the road, and in a few moments found ourselves face to face with the Yankees in full retreat under fire from Glasscock's pistols. In a moment we were locked together.

The entire party was killed or captured with the exception of one officer and two men, who only escaped with fine horses by jumping the fence. In this melee I unhorsed a Yankee sergeant, and shot him through the right shoulder just as he grappled my horse's reins and leveled his pistol in my face. I had the satisfaction to see him roll in the fence corner, but I held captive his horse, a fine sorrel mare, branded U.S., and it was upon this animal I surrendered a few weeks later.

John Hipkins, of Norfolk, Virginia, rode side by side with me, and when we came back up the road, he claimed that he had shot the man. I put the question to the wounded sergeant, who at once pointed to me as the guilty party.

After this little engagement and my participation in the Harmony fight, which took place a few days later, Captain Glasscock suggested that I be made a lieutenant in Baylor's company, then organizing, if I would remain with Mosby's command. It was quite flattering to me to be offered this position, and I should have been only too well pleased to accept it and serve under so gallant a soldier as Baylor, but I was still under orders from Gen. Fitz Lee, and it was my duty to return to that command at the earliest possible moment. I was particularly desirous to be back with my old cavalry chief, and, if surrender had come, to surrender with those with whom I had been associated for several years.

It was just about this time that my cousin, George M. Gill, who had only a few months before joined Mosby's command, went with Lieut. Wiltshire, and several other young men, to make a scout to Stevenson's Depot.

They were approaching the residence of Col. Daniel Bonham, as a Federal officer, who proved to be Lieutenant Eugene Ferris, of the 30th Mass. Infantry, was seen to pass rapidly from the house to the stable, which was situated in the corner of the yard.

Lieut. Wiltshire and my cousin, who were riding fifty yards in advance of their comrades, passing through the gate which admitted them to the yard, dashed up to the stable door in which Ferris was standing. Without drawing his pistol from the holster, Wiltshire demanded a surrender. "Never with life," replied Ferris, and as Wiltshire was in the act of disengaging his pistol, Ferris inflicted a mortal wound in his neck.

Gill immediately fired, but Ferris standing behind the door post was not struck and at once fired on Gill and inflicted on him a disabling wound. By this time the rest of the party had arrived on the scene of combat.

Ferris received a slight wound and was captured. After the encounter was over, my cousin attempted, notwithstanding his wound, to return to his friends at Upperville, but from the loss of blood was compelled to stop at the house of a citizen in the Blue Ridge. I was informed of his whereabouts and went immediately to him. I found him with a serious wound on the left side of his neck, in close proximity to the jugular vein. Although he was brave and cheerful, I realized the danger at once. I told him that I must be off immediately for a doctor, and bring him some clean clothes. I recall very distinctly that it was a Thursday evening. I promised to be back the following evening. I rode all night and on my return Friday night I found my dear cousin a corpse. Oh, the horrors of war! Just as I feared, the wound began to slough. The artery gave way and death followed almost immediately. The last word he uttered, as the old mountaineer stood beside him, who had so carefully cared for him was, "I die at least in a good cause."

We buried him Sunday morning in a little grave-yard on the mountain side. We dug his grave, and I read a portion of the Episcopal burial service as we put him away. His father came after the war and removed his remains to Baltimore, where they now rest at Greenmount. George Gill was an exceptionally fine character. At college he exhibited unusually fine talent for public speaking, a fine omen of success in the practice of law, which would have been his profession had he lived.

He participated in many of the great battles and was everywhere conspicuous for the highest qualities of a soldier. The day after the second battle of Manassas he received a severe wound in a skirmish on the Little River turnpike. This compelled him to absent himself from the army until the middle of November.

From that time until after the disaster at Gettysburg he was constantly with Stuart's cavalry, but was taken prisoner at Hagerstown on the retreat of Lee's army. He spent five dreary months in prison, first at Fort Delaware, then at Point Lookout. At the end of this time he was sent to Richmond, and soon after rejoined his regiment, from which he was transferred to Mosby's Partisan Rangers.

The elements in him were finely blended, for manly courage was united with intelligence, a high morality and great gentleness of disposition.

> *"On Fame's eternal camping ground*
> *Their silent tents are spread,*
> *And memory guards with solemn round*
> *The bivouac of the dead,"*

CHAPTER XI

AFTER A PAROLE, A PRISONER ─────────────

McFarland and I left Mosby's command sometime about the 8th of April, stopping over a few days at Warrenton. Here we learned for the first time of General Lee's surrender to Grant at Appomattox.

The Richmond papers contained his farewell address to his soldiers of that great Army of Northern Virginia, with whom I had marched and fought for more than four years. I am proud of the privilege of having had my name recorded upon such a muster-roll.

General Lee's last words to his soldiers were to cease fighting, return to their homes and strictly observe their parole until exchanged. Here McFarland and I were at Warrenton, greatly perplexed how to decide the next step to be taken. We finally parted at this point. He went to Richmond, where his family resided. I returned to Captain Glasscock's house in Fauquier County. They all welcomed me back, but I brought the sad inevitable news to them, the downfall of the Confederacy.

The next day being Sunday, we all went to church in Upperville, and just as the service was over, some one rode in with a late edition of the Baltimore American, giving full particulars of Lee's surrender and the assassination of President Lincoln.

I think this was about the 16th of April, and the following day copies of General Hancock's proclamation,—who was in command of the Department of the Valley, announcing the surrender of Lee's army and granting to all Confederate soldiers in that locality the same conditions of surrender as had been accorded to Gen. Lee's army, excepting Colonel Mosby, whom they had outlawed, were disseminated through the country.

There was no fighting after this date. Everybody was asking one another what he should do. In discussing the matter with a number of my Maryland comrades I was asked if I intended to accept the terms of surrender and return home. I answered in the affirmative. Everybody was of this opinion, fully realizing that the war was at an end.

It was Sunday, the 23d of April, just after we had finished dinner at Captain Glasscock's house, where it was our custom to lounge on the grass or sit on the fence smoking our pipes, that our attention was called to several horsemen seen in the distance, crossing the fields in our direction. We soon recognized Col. Mosby and several of his men who were with him.

As Col. Mosby rode up, the conversation turned almost immediately to Gen. Hancock's proclamation. He expressed surprise that anyone should accept such terms. He seemed chagrined that I had already advised some of my friends to do so. I soon found that Capt. Glasscock was thoroughly in accord with the views which I had expressed. Mosby protested against any one leaving his territory at that time. Then it was that I told him I had decided to leave Upperville the following morning and proceed with any of my old comrades who would join me to Gen. Hancock's headquarters, to accept the terms of surrender. I was surprised to find about 20 of Mosby's men in the village, all of whom went with me and were duly paroled. The following day Major Richards, with about 300 of Mosby's men rode into Berryville and accepted the same terms.

Those of us who were Marylanders were permitted by Gen. Hancock to go to Harper's Ferry, and from thence proceed by rail to Baltimore over the Baltimore & Ohio Railroad.

When the train arrived at the Relay House late that evening, within 10 miles of Baltimore, and all were feeling exultant over the prospect of getting home that night, we had our feelings very much disturbed by the entrance into the car of a Federal officer demanding the surrender of our paroles. We declined to give them up. He left the car but soon returned with a squad of soldiers, and ordered us out with fixed bayonets. Of course, we obeyed.

We were imprisoned at the Relay House for more than 10 days. As we had been arrested and held as prisoners without explanation, in violation of the sacred pledge of the Government, we felt very much incensed. I finally wrote a letter to General Tyler, then in command at that point, and demanded my release, stating that he had no right to hold me a prisoner, that I had not violated my parole in any way, and that, if I was not to be released, I desired to communicate with my old friend, Mr. Thomas Donaldson, who lived on Lawyer's Hill, and, although a Unionist throughout the war, would see that the wrong was righted and my release secured.

The following morning Gen. Tyler ordered me down under guard to his headquarters. I was told that if I could secure a suit of citizen's clothes from Baltimore, I would be allowed to go into the city.

I asked permission to telegraph to Baltimore, which resulted in getting from Noah Walker & Co., a ready-made suit of clothing, which was sent out to me that afternoon in time for me to return to my family that evening.

Thus ended my four years' experience as a Confederate soldier.

The record of the engagements in which I participated embrace the following historic names:

First Manassas,	Wilderness,
Front Royal,	Sharpsburg,
Winchester,	Gettysburg,
Bolivar Heights,	Strasburg,
Harrisonburg,	Woodstock,
Cross Keys,	Reams's Station,
Seven Days' Battles	Harrison Landing,
Around Richmond,	Hawes Shop,
Cedar Mountain,	Trevilians Station,
Catletts Station,	Yellow Tavern,
Second Manassas,	Brandy Station
Spottsylvania Court House,	and Culpeper,

and many other cavalry engagements.

"Through our great good fortune, in our youth our hearts were touched with fire. It is for us to report to those who come after us."

Justice Oliver Wendell Holmes, Jr.
20th Massachusetts Infantry

BIBLIOGRAPHY

Civil War Times Illustrated, Harrisburg, Pa., 1990.

Dowdey, Clifford, *Lee,* Little, Brown & Co., Boston, 1965.

Faust, Patricia L., Ed., *Encyclopedia of the Civil War,* Harper & Row, New York, 1986.

Field Enterprisers, Inc., *The World Book Encyclopedia,* Chicago, 1957.

Johnson, R. V. and Buel, C. C., *Battles and Leaders of the Civil War,* Vol. IV, The Century Co., New York, 1887.

Milhollen, H. D.; Johnson, J. R.; Bill, A. H.; *Horsemen Blue and Gray,* Oxford University Press, New York, 1960.

Swank, Walbrook D., *Eyewitness to War,* 1861-1865, Papercraft, Inc., Charlottesville, Va., 1990.

Swank, Walbrook D., *The War & Louisa County,* 1861-1865, Papercraft Inc., Charlottesville, Va., 1986.

The Fairfax Press, *The Official Military Atlas of the Civil War,* New York, 1983.

Williamson, James J., *Mosby's Rangers,* R. B. Kenyon, Publisher, New York, 1896.

INDEX

(Names listed with highest rank held.)

MILITARY ORGANIZATIONS